FLY FISHERMAN'S GUIDE TO
SALTWATER PREY

FLY FISHERMAN'S GUIDE TO
Saltwater Prey

Aaron J. Adams, Ph.D.

STACKPOLE BOOKS

Copyright © 2008 by Aaron J. Adams

Published by
STACKPOLE BOOKS
5067 Ritter Road
Mechanicsburg, PA 17055
www.stackpolebooks.com

All rights reserved, including the right to reproduce this book or portions thereof in any form or by any means, electronic or mechanical, including photocopying, recording, or by any information storage and retrieval system, without permission in writing from the publisher. All inquiries should be addressed to Stackpole Books, 5067 Ritter Road, Mechanicsburg, Pennsylvania 17055.

Printed in China

First edition

All photos copyright Aaron J. Adams except where noted.
Cover design by Wendy A. Reynolds.

10 9 8 7 6 5 4 3 2 1

Library of Congress Cataloging-in-Publication Data

Adams, Aaron J.
 Fly fisherman's guide to saltwater prey / Aaron J. Adams.
   p. cm.
 Includes bibliographical references and index.
 ISBN-13: 978-0-8117-3460-8 (alk. paper)
 ISBN-10: 0-8117-3460-9 (alk. paper)
 1. Saltwater fly fishing. 2. Marine fishes—Food. 3. Flies, Artificial. 4. Fly tying.
I. Title.

SH456.2.A33 2008
799.16—dc22
                                                        2007015361

CONTENTS

Acknowledgments vii
Introduction ix

SECTION I: CRABS

1. Mud Crabs: Xanthidae 2
2. Mangrove and Marsh Crabs: Grapsidae 9
3. Fiddler Crabs: Ocypodidae 13
4. Spider Crabs: Majidae 20
5. Porcelain Crabs: Porcellanidae 25
6. Swimming Crabs: Portunidae 26
7. Mole Crabs: Hippidae 40

SECTION II: SHRIMP

8. Common Shrimp: Penaeidae 46
9. Ghost Shrimp and Mud Shrimp:
   Callianassidae and Thalassinidae 59
10. Mantis Shrimp: Squillidae 62
11. Snapping Shrimp: Alpheidae 68
12. Grass Shrimp and Broken-back Shrimp:
    Palaemonidae and Hippolytidae 76

SECTION III: BOTTOM-ASSOCIATED PREY FISH

13. Gobies: Gobiidae 84
14. Blennies: Bleniidae 90
15. Toadfishes: Batrachoididae 95
16. Grunts: Haemulidae 99
17. Snappers: Lutjanidae 103
18. Drums: Sciaenidae 105
19. Porgies: Sparidae 107

SECTION IV: MIDWATER PREY FISH

20 Wrasses and Parrotfishes: Labridae and Scaridae 112
21 Mojarras: Gerreidae 116
22 Killifishes, Mollies, and Mosquitofish:
   Cyprinodontidae and Poecilidae 122
23 Eels: Anguillidae 132

SECTION V: BAITFISH

24 Anchovies: Engraulidae 136
25 Silversides: Atherinidae 141
26 Herrings: Clupeidae 148
27 Needlefishes, Halfbeaks, and Ladyfish:
   Belonidae, Exocoetidae, and Elopidae 162
28 Mullets: Mugilidae 168

SECTION VI: MISCELLANEOUS BOTTOM PREY

29 Segmented Worms: Polychaeta 182
30 Sea Urchins: Echinoidea 187

List of Fly Tiers 189
Bibliography 195
Index 200

ACKNOWLEDGMENTS

No book is ever the work of a single person. People other than the author, whether editors, reviewers, or contributors, have a hand in seeing a book to completion. This is especially true with a book of this nature. Whether by providing feedback as the book idea developed, contributing fly patterns, or helping me with collections and photography of prey, many people had a hand in this book. This is my chance to thank them.

I am grateful to Rick Ruoff and Marshall Cutchin for allowing me the time for some good conversations about the book idea, and providing some sound advice that improved what ended up in these pages. My discussion with Rick on saltwater fly philosophy was especially helpful in clarifying my thoughts, and he will recognize some of the results of that conversation in the introduction. Marshall was especially helpful in providing good, honest feedback on an earlier draft of the book.

My fishing buddies Doug Hedges and Glenn Pittard were helpful in many ways—helping to collect prey, putting up with my photography when we should have been fishing, and contributing numerous fly patterns to the book. I hope they learned some things along the way. Doug had the gut-wrenching experience of watching an angler catch a nice bonefish on a flat while we were sampling. That was tough. I think he understood then why I keep the fly rods at home when I'm collecting—just too much temptation.

Many people contributed flies to the book, and although their names are listed with the patterns they contributed, I think it is important to thank them here as well. After all, they contributed the flies without conditions, trusting me to get the project completed. Fly tiers who contributed to the book are: Ginger Allen, Ken Bay, Tom Berry, Capt. Gordon Churchill, Marshall Cutchin, Capt. Chris Dean, Oscar Feliu, Buz Fender, Les Fulcher, Jack Gartside, Jerry Goldsmith, Capt. Doug Hedges, Andrij Zenon Horodysky, Chris Humphrey, Mike Marsili, Capt. Tony Petrella, Capt. Glenn Pittard, Norman Salesky, Dave Skok, Craig Smothers, Capt. Steve Venini, and Ron Winn.

Collecting and photographing prey was the most time-consuming part of the project, and I benefited from the help of many. My wife, Maria Cochran, endured days pulling nets, and my parents, Joe and Sandy, also helped on numerous days. Also deserving thanks are Kirby Wolfe, Vero's Sport and Tackle Shop, Alex Anderson, Craig Dahlgren, Andy Danylchuk, Phil Kramer, and Carlton "Captain" Westby Jr. I also thank the folks at Stackpole Books for improving my functional photography to better present the prey and the flies and especially Amy Lerner for getting this book into shape.

Jon Lucy and Chris and Spud Woodward were helpful with information on fish diets. Many people helped with prey identification or pointing me in the right direction in my search for identification keys. Thanks to Dave Blewett, Patrick Casey, Chuck Idelberger, Greg Tolley, Anamari Boyes, and Jim Van Tassell. Despite their best intentions, I'm sure I've made errors in identification, for which I take sole responsibility.

And finally, I thank the many fly anglers whose positive response to my presentations at their fly clubs convinced me to, once again, take some time away from fishing and put this book together. Photos of prey and flies were the most well-received part of my presentations, and I came to realize that many anglers were creating new flies based solely on my descriptions of prey in my first book, *Fisherman's Coast*. I hope this book meets their expectations.

INTRODUCTION

Many of today's saltwater fly tiers have become incredibly adept at creating flies that closely mimic the many species of prey eaten by coastal gamefish. In fact, there are some very good books of saltwater fly patterns, and these books provide an abundance of fly selections for saltwater anglers. But when it comes to selecting flies to put in the fly box for a day of fishing, or for a fishing trip away from our home waters, we tend to rely on our hunches, or on selecting flies that look fishy. This tends to happen when creating and modifying fly patterns too. What our selection process lacks is the connection between our flies and what gamefish are actually eating, and where and when they are doing it. The purpose of this book is to shed some light on gamefish prey so that this information can be incorporated into our fly-tying and selection process, and making these processes easier.

As a biologist who spends many hours in the field studying fish behavior, biology, and habitat, I think I have a little different insight into gamefish and their prey than most anglers. Even when fishing, my natural tendency is to put as much effort into visually assessing all of the things that surround fishing—habitats, prey, predators, fish behavior, tide, wind, temperature, etc.—as much as I do into actually fishing and catching. Regardless of whether I catch the fish or not, I take a step back, put all the surrounding factors into consideration, and make a guess as to why I did or didn't catch the fish.

Despite my constant study of gamefish and their worlds, I remain astounded at the variety of prey types they have to choose from, and the daily, seasonal, and yearly changes these prey undergo. Juvenile blue crabs, for example, are high on the prey menu of many coastal gamefish, but they tend to be most abundant in the correct size range for only part of the year and in only a few habitats.

Another example of changes in prey preference can be found in common snook (*Centropomus undecimalis*), whose diet differs depending on the season and the habitat they are occupying. For example, in Florida, although juvenile pinfish (*Lagodon rhomboides*) approximately 1 inch long are very abundant during early spring, snook rarely eat them. But in late spring, when the pinfish have grown to 3 inches, they jump up to number one on the snook menu. And when snook are feeding in mangrove creeks, they tend to eat small (1 inch–3 inches), earth-colored killifishes, aka mud minnows (family Cyprinodontidae), and silvery mojarras (family Gerreidae), whereas in more open habitats shrimp (family Penaeidae), silversides (family Engraulidae), and anchovies (family Atherinidae) top the list of prey. In these examples you have the essence of this book—this knowledge allows fly anglers to create, tie, and select flies based on the habitat, location, and season they are fishing.

The dynamics of saltwater prey is easily as complex as the cycle of insect species that appear on a spring creek throughout the course of a year, but this has not yet been truly acknowledged in the general fly-fishing world. Perhaps this is why saltwater fly anglers generally do not have the same level of insight into what saltwater gamefish are eating, and why, as do trout anglers. This book provides some of that insight for coastal gamefish by showing you the dominant prey and where they can most often be found, and by presenting flies that have been successful at mimicking these prey at the right time and place. There is no need to go out and examine gamefish stomach contents or to do the habitat studies to determine which prey are available—that's all been done. What this book will do, I hope, is help you discover, and better understand, a system for determining what flies to tie and when to use them. This book presents the prey and flies from the gamefish's perspective: in which habitats are these prey found, in what regions, during which seasons, at what sizes, and which version of a fly (e.g., weighted or unweighted) is most appropriate for a habitat.

One of my intentions with this book is to encourage saltwater fly anglers and fly tiers to think outside the box that so many of us have created for ourselves. We need to do less selecting of flies from an angler's perspective, and do a better job of selecting from the gamefish's perspective. Knowing why a pattern is good for a particular situation will also help an angler present the fly in the most appropriate fashion. Attractor patterns aside, our trout angling brethren tend to choose their flies based on the conditions at hand, the same conditions the trout must interpret to find and eat prey while remaining safe from predators. Many of the fly-pattern books for trout anglers are presented with this in mind, and many trout anglers have become amateur entomologists (and better anglers) in the process. This doesn't mean that saltwater anglers have to be able to identify prey to the exact species, but they are certainly better off knowing what prey are present, and which are most often eaten by gamefish, so they are able to more closely "match the hatch."

Fly selection is not the only important factor. How the fly is presented is at least as important. A small white Deceiver, for example, might be perfect for imitating prey along the beach as well as mangroves, but the fly used while fishing along mangroves should have a weedguard and should perhaps even be tied bendback style. That is the fly selection component. The fly presentation component involves how the fly is fished. Along mangroves, which provide a rather narrow area of ambush habitat for gamefish, I think it's best to work the fly slowly, with short, erratic strips, maybe even just twitches. In contrast, when fishing this fly over seagrass, I like to keep the fly moving just over the top of the seagrass blades. These presentations not only give gamefish the maximum opportunity to attack the fly, they also mimic the typical behavior of small prey fish in these habitats.

Whether or not a fly is weighted is also an important factor to consider in fly design and presentation. One of my favorite flies for tailing bonefish is a small tan crab pattern, a modified version of Del Brown's Merkin. But I use two versions of this fly—weighted for water greater than 10-inch depth or on rough days, and unweighted for when fish are tailing in skinny water or on calm days. I can let this fly settle slowly to the bottom, where the fish sees it, or strip it slowly through midwater, like a swimming crab (family Portunidae) trying to flee the scene. In deeper water the weighted fly gets to the bottom quickly, so it probably imitates a swimming crab shooting downward to hide in the bottom. The fly can be presented in either fashion, and if the fly and presentation match the conditions, the bonefish will react aggressively.

This book is intended as a complement to *Fisherman's Coast* (Stackpole Books, 2004), which explained coastal habitats and prey from the gamefishes' perspective. I think this a genuinely different approach than has been typical in saltwater fishing to date. An angler who understands the workings of the gamefish's world is more likely to put him or herself in the right place at the right time to find fish, and this was the focus of *Fisherman's Coast*. I intend for *Fly Fisherman's Guide to Saltwater Prey* to be the next step—to encourage saltwater anglers to think about, create, tie, and use fly patterns that are appropriate for the conditions they are fishing, and to fish the flies in a manner that mimics the appropriate prey. In other words, *Fisherman's Coast* told you about gamefish habitats and prey, *Fly Fisherman's Guide to Saltwater Prey* shows you the prey and fly patterns.

As in *Fisherman's Coast*, this book is specific to warm-temperate, subtropical, and tropical regions. Prey species from each of the families listed here, however, are also present in other regions, and the tactics I offered in *Fisherman's Coast* and the flies that are presented here are also effective on gamefish in other regions. Thus, a creative angler should be able to adapt patterns and fishing strategies to locations outside the coverage of this book.

You will note numerous references within this book to specific habitat types, such as low marsh, black mangrove shorelines, and different species of seagrass. In all cases, these habitat types, and how gamefish use them, are fully covered in *Fisherman's Coast*, and that information is not repeated here.

As in *Fisherman's Coast,* I use scientific names to identify the prey species, in part to reduce confusion caused by popular regional names. For example, scaled sardines (*Harengula jaguana*) are also called whitebait (Florida west coast) and pilchards (Florida east coast), and Atlantic thread herring (*Opisthonema oglinum*) are often called greenies and greenbacks. In addition, scientific names are more useful if you want to conduct your own research on prey. You will find much more (and more accurate) information using the scientific names than using local common names.

THE PREY

There are many thousands of fish and invertebrates that are potential prey for coastal gamefish. Many gamefish are opportunistic enough that they likely at least sample a fair number of these prey at some point in their lives. This huge array of potential prey can be overwhelming for an angler trying to choose flies for a day of fishing. But as any angler can tell you, each gamefish species has a main menu from which they most often eat, while occasionally sampling the sides. One of the challenges in putting this book together was to narrow down this very large list of potential prey to a list of most likely to be eaten by coastal gamefish. I did this in two ways: first, by collecting scientific articles on diets of gamefish, which you will find listed in the bibliography; and second, by observation—my own observations of gamefish stomach contents, and conversations with anglers and biologists about their observations.

But don't think that scientific studies of gamefish diet are the end-all. Even these studies require some interpretation to determine which listed prey are worthwhile for imitation with a fly. Bonefish, for example, eat a lot of clams (especially bonefish less than 16 inches fork length), but tying a clam fly, much less trying to fish it, is not worthwhile. Similarly, red drum eat sixty or more species of prey, but many of these prey are either not appropriate for imitation with a fly or occur in habitats that are generally not fished by fly anglers (e.g., open bottom 10 feet deep). So when examining scientific studies of gamefish diets, my first steps were to determine which prey species are appropriate for imitation with a fly and which prey species are most abundant in habitats frequented by fly anglers. This led to the next step—to know or learn enough about the habitat requirements of the prey to determine in which habitats the scientific studies occurred. Were the gamefish collected in seagrass, salt marsh, or open bottom habitats, for example? This is not clear in many studies. In addition, the availability of prey and the habitat uses and behaviors of gamefish interact to cause seasonal changes in diet, which I had to piece together from other studies of prey abundance in habitats and my own experiences. Some scientific diet studies do this (that is, they use seasonality or habitat as factors in the study), but many don't. Once again, some knowledge of the seasonality of prey and of gamefish behavior was necessary to boil this information down to something useful from a fly angler's perspective. Finally, I had to factor in that the diets of many gamefish species vary among locations; some of this results from differences in prey availability and some from differences in habitats. South Carolina, for example, has no seagrass, so red drum live and feed mostly in association with salt marsh habitats, whereas red drum in much of Florida are often found feeding in or near seagrass beds. All of these factors were important when I was culling the list of potential prey for this book.

Another very important factor was observation of gamefish stomachs and feeding. I examined the stomach contents of red drum feeding in seagrass beds in my home waters in southwest Florida, for example, and found (in order from most to least abundant): mud crabs (often the common mud crab, *Panopeus herbstii*), snapping shrimp (genus *Alpheus*), and small gobies (family Gobiidae) and blennies (family Blenniidae). In contrast, I found that red drum feeding on mud flats adjacent to black mangrove shorelines ate mostly fiddler crabs and juvenile blue crabs. My observations differed from a scientific article describing red drum diet as being fish-dominated. The differences between my observations and the study were because the study captured red drum primarily from deeper, more open water habitats, but I was sampling shallow seagrass beds and muddy shorelines. This is not to say that red drum don't eat fish; they eat a lot of fish, but the scientific study missed a significant portion of the red drum diet that can be exploited by fly anglers because of where the sampling occurred.

I also benefited from conversations with numerous anglers and biologists over the years. Although anecdotal, these eyewitness accounts of gamefish feeding behavior and stomach contents were useful in many cases when I was deciding whether a particular prey should be included in the book. In fact, in a couple cases these conversations caused me to include prey that would not otherwise be in the book.

I think that all of the prey listed within this book are eaten frequently enough that they are worthy of imitation with flies. You will note, however, that not all prey species are shown in photographs. This is partly because many species are very similar in appearance, so multiple photographs are not worthwhile. But this is mostly because collecting some species was more difficult than I anticipated. This does not mean these species are not abundant, many are, rather that they were difficult to collect. It is also my own bias that artist renderings of prey generally do not do the species justice in the sense of an image useful for tying flies. After all, there is naturally some of the artist's own interpretation of the prey in their reproduction, much the same as the artistic license taken by fly tiers when they create a fly to mimic a prey. Thus, I opted not to use drawings for species lacking photos. Drawings or photos of most of these species are available in some of the references listed at the end of the book.

To the extent possible, the prey shown in this book were photographed alive. I think this is important because live photos are most likely to show true coloration of the prey and, as important, to show the prey's true form (extended fins or legs) when in the water. Photographing these prey in the field, however, is a challenge—some prey never stop moving, lighting is always tough, weather is often not cooperative, and conditions in remote locations are often not the best.

When possible, prey were photographed in a V-shaped aquarium. I filled the bottom of the aquarium with epoxy or silicone to prevent prey from wedging themselves into the V—although this had the benefit of forcing bottom-dwelling prey to rest upright, it had the disadvantage of making for a less attractive photograph. I opted for functional photographs of prey and kept the epoxy in the aquarium. In cases where the prey were too active and wouldn't stay still for a photograph in the aquarium, they were most often held in the palm of a hand. For many of the mud crabs, their shape and behavior (they constantly tried to ball up in the corner of the aquarium), I found that placing them on a flat surface worked best. All that said, I believe strongly in function over form, and all of the photographs are functional.

THE FLIES

Ask experienced fly anglers and most will tell you that presentation is perhaps the most important factor in catching gamefish on fly. Many anglers take this response to mean getting the fly to a spot where the fish can see it without spooking the fish. But getting the fly to the right spot on time is only part of the presentation. The other part of the presentation is giving the fly the action that goads a gamefish to strike. So the fly must not only have appropriate physical prey characteristics, but must also move like a prey. How the angler manipulates the fly is a key component in the presentation, but the fly must first be composed of the right materials and tied in the correct fashion to be presented in the appropriate habitat. In this light, in each prey section I provide general information on prey behavior—information important to how a fly is tied and fished.

In general, I think fly-tying strategy can be broken down into two types—impressionistic and imitation. Both strategies can be effective, and often a mixture of impressionistic and imitation yields the best results. I move back and forth between these two extremes but generally put myself more to the side of impressionistic fly tiers. I use my understanding of the gamefish and their habitats in an attempt to figure out which prey characteristics trigger a feeding response from gamefish. I then try to incorporate these characteristics into a fly pattern, with less attention to imitating a particular prey species. Size, action, and color are the main factors I use in tying flies. I also must admit that I generally tie simple flies. I like to tie flies, but I prefer to be on the water fishing those flies, so more often than not I tie with a purpose—my preferred patterns are those that I can tie many of in one sitting, stocking the box for the next day of fishing.

The Mangrove Muddler, presented in this book, meets my standards for an impressionistic, simple fly. It is a simplified saltwater adaptation of the standard muddler, but tied appropriately it presents a good impression of the killifishes, mollies, and mosquitofishes that are so prevalent in mangrove and salt marsh habitats. Tied to the leader with a loop knot, the sparse tail and deer hair head cause the fly to wobble just under the surface, closely resembling the movements of many species of mudminnows. The Mangrove Muddler has become my favorite fly for fishing in these habitats, regardless of the gamefish. The Mangrove Muddler is also an example of my tendency to "oversize" many of my flies in relation to the naturals. Many of the prey listed in this book don't grow very large, and at times a fly of the same size may not be noticed by a gamefish. Without overdoing it, I think that tying slightly larger representations of the prey not only increases the chances of being noticed by the gamefish, it also elicits a more energetic strike—a tasty morsel too good to pass up.

In contrast, the studious observation, creativity, and persistence required to tie exacting prey imitations becomes an art in itself, and often pays off on the water. Imitation fly tiers are able to incorporate the morphological and visual characteristics of gamefish prey into flies that can also be manipulated by the angler to move like the prey. For these tiers, careful reproduction of prey shape and size, as well as color pattern, are key components to fly creation. Imitations that lack malleability, however, even though they may be dead ringers for the prey they are imitating, tend to catch fewer fish.

Ken Bay's Pinfish patterns are great examples of successful imitations. Pinfish are important prey for numerous gamefish in subtropical and warm-temperate climates, so are good subjects of fly imitation. Ken's patterns are dead ringers for pinfish—true in size, shape, and color—but are also tied with materials that provide an illusion of movement. These have been successful and popular flies for Ken.

Another key component to the good flies is that they are castable and fishable. They are not overburdened with materials. Even flies that appear large are not tied large. In other words, materials are used sparingly so that the fly can be cast with a fly rod, but give the impression of bulk. Sparsely tied flies tend to "breathe" better, thus giving additional motion to the fly. And sparse materials on baitfish flies create a translucence that, when viewed in the water, gives the impression of light reflecting off scales. Dave Skok, who tied numerous patterns for this book, is a master of this skill.

I think that many of the prey groups are underrepresented by flies to imitate them. In most cases, I think this is because fly anglers don't know about these prey. I call these the untapped prey for gamefish—species that gamefish eat frequently but that aren't exploited by most fly tiers and anglers. Blennies, gobies, and toadfish, for example, are all eaten by gamefish (bonefish, snook, red drum, spotted seatrout, among others), but only rarely have I seen other anglers using flies to imitate these prey. To some extent, I think flies that have traditionally been used as shrimp imitations have actually been mistaken for other (less obvious) prey by gamefish. My guess is that many of the weighted, furry-bodied flies with barred tails, which are so often used by anglers as shrimp imitations, are taken by gamefish as bottom-dwelling fish like gobies, blennies, or toadfish. Many of these patterns generally look like these prey fishes, and the ways they are most effectively fished imitates the behaviors of these prey. Many other prey listed in this book are similarly untapped by fly anglers. Hopefully, this book will give anglers and tiers a new perspective in this regard.

You will also note that some prey groups contain no flies. Despite the lack of flies contributed by tiers for the book (myself included), I retained these prey groups in the hope that their inclusion would spur the creation of flies by readers of the book. These prey *are* eaten by gamefish.

Finally, in areas with murky water, where gamefish are more likely to feel the fly with their lateral line system or hear the fly with their inner ear, tiers may want to concentrate on flies that take advantage of these senses. Flies that push a lot of water, for example, send out small pressure waves that are sensed by the lateral line, and clue a gamefish to the presence of the fly. Muddler- and Seaducer-style flies have this property. Poppers and flies with rattles take advantage of the fact that sound travels nearly five times faster in water than in air, allowing a fly to "call" a fish in from a greater distance. This is one reason I like the Phat Phoam Gurgler as an all-around searching fly in blind-casting situations.

THE FLY TIERS

It can be fascinating to peek into the fly boxes of fellow saltwater fly anglers, especially those with an intimate familiarity with their gamefish quarry. An angler's fly box represents an accumulation of knowledge gained over countless hours on (or even in) the water. For those less practiced, such a peek into a fly box shortens the learning curve. This I learned early on—if you want to learn what a professional tier uses on the water, don't focus on what he/she ties for the fly shops; sneak a look into his/her fly box. This book provides just such a peek.

You will find a mixture of original, established, long-standing standards, and modified patterns in this book—the best flies for the task at hand. The key is that all of these flies are being presented in the context of specific prey groups—in other words, they are presented in a fishing context—what prey they best imitate and in what habitats they are best fished, which provide clues to best ways to present the flies to fish. Some patterns you will have seen in shops, so the fact that they appear here is a testament to their effectiveness.

I invited multiple tiers to tie patterns as a window into the minds of anglers who spend a lot of time on the water and at the vise, and who tie flies based on their experience and the understanding they have for coastal habitats and gamefish. And, quite frankly, I knew I would be unable to give justice to the more than one hundred prey species covered in this book relying on only my tying skills and imagination. I purposefully did not assign tiers specific prey or fly patterns. In this way, I have incorporated some redundancy into the book. I think redundancy in fly patterns can be a good thing—it helps us see how to imitate prey through multiple tier's perspectives, and see which prey characteristics tiers think are most important. One tier may focus on characteristics of a prey species that I also see, while another tier may highlight a subtlety that I would have otherwise missed. Creativity and interpretation are infinite. Brief biographies of many fly tiers are included to give a personal side to the flies. Allowing tiers to tie flies of their choice also underscores the lack of attention for the "untapped" prey groups that are presented in this book.

After much thought, I have decided not to enter the controversy of identifying a fly's originator, so pattern originators are presented at the discretion of the tiers. In some debate, I decided to include information for these species. Photographs aside, I think that knowledge of the varieties of prey available to gamefish (and available to tiers for imitating with new flies) gives anglers better insight into their quarry. In addition, I hope that there is enough interest in this book that a second edition with additional photographs and flies is warranted.

Identification of some species can be difficult, especially species that are similar in appearance. Counting the number of fin rays, for example, is a typical way to distinguish many species of anchovies. Even more difficult for a fish-focused biologist like me is identification of some of the invertebrates. Mud crabs and fiddler crabs, for example, are often identified by the configuration of the inner portions of the claws. I did my best to identify all species featured in this book, but I'm sure I've made mistakes, for which I take full responsibility. Fortunately, I don't see my errors having an effect on fly tiers.

SECTION I
Crabs

CHAPTER 1

Mud Crabs
Xantidae

Prey Type: Bottom-associated crabs
Primary Habitats: Seagrass, oyster bars, beachrock shorelines, salt marsh, mangroves
Geographic Range: Mud crabs occur in warm-temperate, subtropical, and tropical regions
Comments: Mud crabs are generally small, so care must be taken to tie flies of appropriate size (it's common for tiers to tie mud crab imitations that are too large). Most of the mud crabs I've found in red drum stomachs I've examined, for example, have been the size of a nickel, a few the size of a quarter. This is also true for bonefish. This size range dominates, even though many species of mud crabs grow larger.

Most mud crabs are not fast movers. If they do move quickly, it's only for short distances—they are quick to scurry to the undersides of oyster shells or rocks when chased. They are also closely associated with the bottom. These behavior characteristics should give you clues on how to present mud crab flies to gamefish. Red drum, bonefish, and mutton snapper are probably the primary gamefish predators of mud crabs, though I'm certain permit, snook, and spotted seatrout will take a well-presented mud crab fly.

Many species of mud crabs are similar in overall appearance to many species of spider crabs (family Majidae, chapter 4). Thus, many of the crab patterns shown here and in chapter 4 are interchangeable. I've also found that an appropriately presented Del Brown's Merkin (tied in green and/or brown) is a good bet for imitating mud crabs.

Species: Common Mud Crab

Panopeus herbstii

Primary Habitats: Open mud bottom, oyster bars, salt marsh
Geographic Range: New England to Florida, Gulf of Mexico, Caribbean
Size Range: to $1^3/4$ inches
Comments: True to its name, this is probably the most common mud crab species in open bottom, oyster bar, and marsh habitats, and even seagrass.

Photo on page 1: Fiddler crab holes along a mangrove-edged shoreline.

Species: Say's Mud Crab
Neopanope sayi

Primary Habitats: Open mud bottom, seagrass, oyster bars
Geographic Range: New England to south Florida
Size Range: to 1 inch
Comments: A similar species, the Texas mud crab, *Neopanope texana*, is nearly identical in appearance to Say's mud crab but is found in the northern Gulf of Mexico.

Species: Depressed Mud Crab
Eurypanopeus depressus

Primary Habitats: Open mud bottom, seagrass, oyster bars
Geographic Range: New England to Florida, Caribbean
Size Range: to $7/10$ inch
Comments: This species is the most abundant on intertidal and shallow subtidal oyster bars of the Gulf of Mexico and southeastern U.S. Atlantic coast.

Species: Narrow Mud Crab
Hexapanopeus angustifrons

Primary Habitats: Mud bottom, sand bottom with shell
Geographic Range: New England to Florida, Gulf of Mexico, Caribbean
Size Range: to $4/5$ inch

Mud Crabs (Xantidae)

Species: Florida Mud Crab

Cataleptodius floridanus
(and three other nearly identical species)

Primary Habitats: Mud bottom
Geographic Range: Florida, Caribbean
Size Range: to ⁷/₈ inch

Species: Denticulate Mud/Rubble Crab

Xantho denticulata

Primary Habitats: Rocky and rubble shoreline
Geographic Range: South Florida, Caribbean
Size Range: to 1 inch

Species: Stone Crab

Menippe mercenaria
(juvenile size only)

Primary Habitats: Oyster bars
Geographic Range: North Carolina to Florida, Gulf of Mexico
Size Range: Juveniles to 1 inch
Comments: Adult stone crabs are too much for gamefish to handle, but the juveniles live in the same habitats and are similar in size and coloration to mud crabs.

Here are unidentified mud crab species from warm-temperate and subtropical oyster reefs.

These are unidentified mud crab species from tropical beachrock and rubble shorelines.

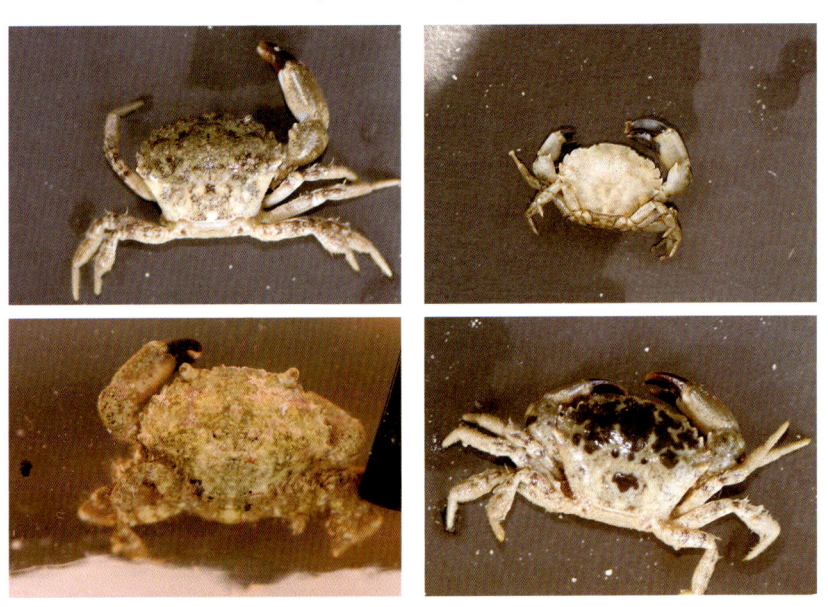

Mud Crabs (Xantidae)

FLIES

Prey Species: Mud Crab
Fly Pattern: Green Mud Crab
Fly Type: Imitation

TIER: AARON ADAMS

Hook: Mustad 34007, size 4
Claws: Olive grizzly hackle
Legs: Olive Sili Legs
Body: Olive wool, spun
Weight: Dumbbell
Thread: Danville flat waxed nylon, olive
Weedguard: 30-pound-test Ande monofilament

Tier Comments: I learned this pattern from a fellow angler back in the late 1990s. I don't remember his name, but I do remember he was from Oregon and fished a lot in Belize. We crossed paths in the British Virgin Islands. It's been a solid pattern in numerous situations.

Mud crabs tend to be slow movers, so a presentation that is close to the fish and little movement of the fly are key to this pattern's success. Adding a tuft of marabou between the hackle claws may provide enough movement to get a nonmoving fly noticed by a gamefish.

Prey Species: Mud Crab
Fly Pattern: Mud Crab Pulverizer
Fly Type: Impressionistic

TIER: GINGER ALLEN

Hook: Mustad 34007, size 1 or 2
Tail: White calf tail, gold flash, four brown/black lace hackle splayed out, two brown/black lace furnace hackle palmered
Body: Clear acetate plastic diamond, weighted with micro split shot on sides, coated with epoxy mixed with gold Pulver dust
Thread: Gudebrod G, black

Tier Comments: This fly was originated by George Phillips and Jerry Martin and is designed to ride hook point up.

Prey Species: Mud Crab
Fly Pattern: Pompom Crab
Fly Type: Impressionistic

TIER: GLENN PITTARD

Hook: C47SD, size 1, or Mustad 34007, size 4
Body: 10 mm pom-pom—color to suit
Legs: Rubber legs
Eyes: 25-pound-test Mason monofilament
Tail: Hackle, rabbit fur, or marabou

Tying Instructions
1. Crush barb and skewer pom-pom onto hook point; push around hook bend and forward to hook eye.
2. Start a thread base at the hook shank; attach hackles for a wing. Next attach two pieces of Mason monofilament with ends melted for eyes and color them black with either paint or marker. Palmer a hackle over the thread wraps.
3. Dab some Zap-Gel or other glue over edge of thread wraps and hook shank, slide pom-pom back into place, and allow glue to hold in place.
4. Once pom-pom is secure, legs can be attached. Using a sewing needle, thread a rubber leg through the pom-pom body. I like the look of three sets.
5. Body can be colored with permanent marker if preferred.

Tier Comments: This fly can be tied with bead chain or barbell eyes if a faster sink rate is desired. However, the pom-pom absorbs water, which gives it a naturally quicker sink rate, so I prefer to fish it unweighted. It can be tied in a variety of colors depending on the habitat and location being fished.

Prey Species: Mud Crab (or small spider crabs)
Fly Pattern: Critter Crab
Fly Type: Impressionistic

TIER: CHRIS DEAN

Hook: Mustad 34007, size 4
Butt: Orange sparkle chenille tied in just past the bend of the hook
Eyes: Burnt monofilament, 30-pound-test Mason
Hackle: Brown neck hackle
Body: Tan Aunt Lydia's rug yarn, five pieces; after tying, comb out the yarn and trim to shape; color the top of the body with an olive marker
Weight: mini lead eyes
Thread: flat waxed nylon, white
Weedguard: 20-pound-test Mason monofilament, single piece tied in aft of the lead eyes

Tier Comments: This is my favorite fly for tailing bonefish. I've been using this fly since 1993. It's a Tim Borski design, with some minor changes. I use rug yarn instead of ram's wool and position the weedguard aft of the lead eyes.

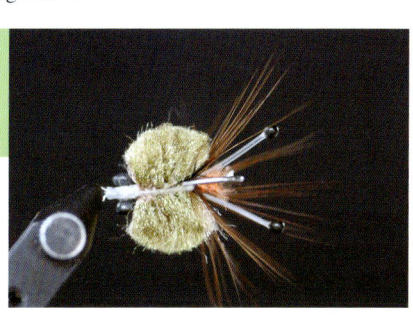

Prey Species: Mud Crab
Fly Pattern: Steve's Sheepshead Crab
Fly Type: Impressionistic

TIER: AARON ADAMS

Hook: Mustad 34007, size 8
Legs: Olive Sili Legs
Body: Olive chenille, medium, one wrap on each side and at the juncture of the legs
Weight: Medium bead chain
Thread: Danville flat waxed nylon, olive

Tying Instructions
1. Tie in the bead chain eyes, and move the thread to the hook bend.
2. Tie in the chenille; move the thread to midshank.
3. Tie in the legs with a couple figure-eight wraps.
4. Wrap the chenille forward, one wrap behind the legs, one wrap over the leg crossing point, one wrap between the legs and bead chain eyes.
5. Tie off, trim, and whip-finish. It doesn't really matter which direction the legs point, as long as they splay outward.

Tier Comments: This pattern was shown to me by Key Largo guide Capt. Steve Venini, who uses it for sight-casting to sheepshead on the flats.

Prey Species: Mud Crab
Fly Pattern: Jerry's Critter
Fly Type: Impressionistic

TIER: JERRY GOLDSMITH

Hook: Mustad 34007, size 4
Claws: Orange grizzly hackle, two on each side
Collar: Palmered orange grizzly hackle
Eyes: Puglisi crab and shrimp eyes
Antennae: Orange Krystal Flash
Mouth Parts: Orange Krystal Flash
Body: Orange cactus chenille
Thread: Danville flat waxed nylon, black

CHAPTER 2

Mangrove and Marsh Crabs
Grapsidae

Prey Type: Marsh- and mangrove-associated crabs
Primary Habitats: Marsh and mangrove shorelines
Geographic Range: Marsh crabs occur in warm-temperate, subtropical, and tropical regions
Comments: Flies imitating these species are appropriate in very specific situations—along mangrove shorelines with vegetation overhanging the water (mangrove tree crabs), and mangrove and marsh shorelines with oyster shell (marsh crabs).

The marsh crabs (purple, marbled, and gray) are generally slow movers and are found near the high tide line, often associated with oyster shell. Darker crab patterns fished slowly are good selections to imitate these species.

Red drum and bonefish are probably the primary gamefish predators of these crabs, but I know that snook occasionally eat them, and I imagine that opportunistic spotted seatrout and permit would as well.

Species: Mangrove Tree Crab

Aratus pisonii

Primary Habitats: Mangroves
Geographic Range: South Florida, Caribbean
Size Range: to 1 inch
Comments: The mangrove tree crab lives on the branches of mangroves and occasionally falls into the water (or intentionally drops off limbs to avoid predators). Gamefish cruising along mangrove shorelines that hear the plop of the crab hitting the water often investigate. The mangrove tree crab can scurry toward the mangrove shoreline across or just under the water surface, or drop to the bottom, search out a prop root, and climb back above the water. Although they can certainly move through the water, because their rearmost legs lack the paddles found on swimming crabs (family Portunidae), they do not move rapidly. In general, long, slow strips work best for flies imitating this crab.

Species: Purple Marsh Crab

Sesarma reticulatum

Primary Habitats: Salt marsh and tidal creek shorelines, sometimes mixed with fiddler crabs
Geographic Range: New England to Florida, Gulf of Mexico
Size Range: to 1 inch

Species: Marbled Marsh Crab

Sesarma ricordi

Primary Habitats: Near the high tide line of mangrove shorelines, among oyster shells
Geographic Range: Tropics
Size Range: to 1 inch

Species: Gray Marsh Crab

Sesarma cinereum

Primary Habitats: Oyster bars and rubble in salt marshes near high tide line
Geographic Range: Mid-Atlantic to Florida
Size Range: to $^{3}/_{4}$ inch

FLIES

Prey Species: Mangrove Tree Crab
Fly Pattern: Splat Crab
Fly Type: Imitation

TIER: AARON ADAMS

Hook: Mustad 34007, size 1
Body: Tan fly foam, cut to shape, one piece each on top and bottom of hook shank
Legs: Rubber band
Eyes: Burned 30-pound-test monofilament
Thread: Flat waxed nylon, tan
Tying Instructions
1. Coat the hook shank with thread to provide a better gripping surface for the glue.
2. After cutting the top and bottom body pieces to shape, put a coating of Goop or similar product on one body piece that is lying flat on the fly-tying bench.
3. Arrange the legs and eyes on this piece of foam, leaving a space down the middle for the hook shank.
4. Lay the hook shank, hook point up, on the Gooped body foam.
5. Place the second piece of body foam on top (you may need to add more Goop).

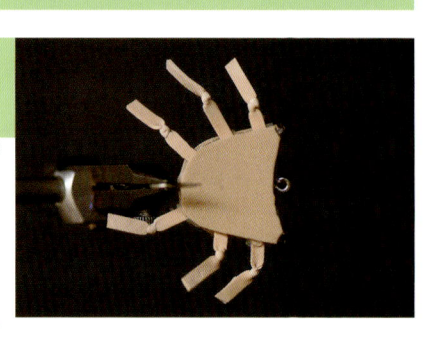

6. Gently squeeze the pieces together and set aside to dry.
7. When dry, color top with permanent markers, but leave the bottom uncolored.

Tier Comments: True to its name, this pattern is designed to land on the water with a splat, mimicking the sound made when tree crabs fall off mangrove branches into the water. It should be fished slowly, with very short, halting strips near the mangrove edge, and then recast.

Prey Species: Marsh Crab
Fly Pattern: Petrella's Crab
Fly Type: Impressionistic

TIER: TONY PETRELLA

Hook: Mustad 34011, size 4
Body: Deer hair dyed dark brown and trimmed to shape
Eyes: Large red bead chain
Butt: Orange estaz
Claws: One furnace hackle or one partridge feather per side with several strands of gold Krystal Flash and a small clump of bucktail dyed dark brown between the feathers
Face: Orange estaz wrapped in a figure eight over and between the eyes
Thread: 3/0 monocord, brown

Prey Species: Marsh Crab
Fly Pattern: EAP
Fly Type: Impressionistic

TIER: AARON ADAMS

Hook: Mustad 34007, size 2
Body: Black and purple Puglisi fibers, tied Merkin-style
Eyes: Medium bead chain, painted black—tied in at the hook bend
Legs: Black rubber
Thread: Flat waxed nylon, black
Weedguard: 30-pound-test monofilament

Tying Tips: I like to use Puglisi fibers for this pattern rather than yarn—the fly lasts longer and can be retrimmed when it gets too bushy. Pull a small bunch of Puglisi fibers off the main bundle, and roll it between your thumb and fingers so that it looks like a stretch of yarn. Clip the rolled fiber bundle to appropriate lengths, and tie in as with a standard Merkin pattern (fiber bundles laid perpendicular to the hook shank, tied in with a figure eight). I tie the fiber bundles with spaces between them (unlike the Merkin, where I pack them in), so only tie in five bundles on the hook shank. Unlike in the Merkin, in this pattern the legs are tied to the hook shank between the Puglisi fiber tie-in spots. The final step is to trim the body to the boxy shape of a marsh crab.

Tier Comments: The name of this fly is an acronym for Edgar Allen Poe. I am a Baltimore Ravens fan. Their colors are black and purple, and their name is from Poe's famous poem "The Raven"—Poe spent considerable time in Baltimore and is buried there. This fly is best fished by casting close to an oyster shoreline, letting the fly drop, with a few short strips, and then recasting.

Prey Species: Marsh Crab
Fly Pattern: Marsh Crab
Fly Type: Impressionistic

TIER: AARON ADAMS

Hook: Mustad 34007, size 2
Underbody: Lavender bucktail
Overbody: White Furry Foam, colored with a permanent marker
Weight: Medium bead chain, painted black—tied in at the hook bend
Legs: Round rubber legs, colored with permanent marker
Thread: Flat waxed nylon, black

Tying Instructions
1. Tie in the legs with figure-eight knots, midshank, on the underside of the shank.
2. Tie in the bead chain eyes on the underside of the hook shank, near the hook bend.
3. Tie in the bucktail on the hook-point side of the shank.
4. Cut the Furry Foam to shape and color the top side.
5. Tie the narrow end of the Furry Foam to the hook shank, on the hook-point side, just in front of the bead chain eyes. Whip-finish.
6. Put a small spot of glue on the underside of the Furry Foam and press it down onto the bucktail. This prevents the Furry Foam from fouling on the hook.

Prey Species: Mangrove Tree Crab
Fly Pattern: Charlie's Floating Crab
Fly Type: Impressionistic

TIER: AARON ADAMS

Hook: Tiemco TMC 811s or Mustad 34007, size 2
Underbody: $1/8$-inch fly foam, tan
Overbody: $1/8$-inch fly foam, white, colored with a permanent marker
Eyes: Burned 40-pound-test monofilament, ends blackened with a permanent marker
Legs: Purple grizzly hackle
Thread: Flat waxed nylon

Tying Tips: This pattern is put together entirely with glue (Zap-A-Gap). After laying a thread base on the hook shank, the parts are assembled in this order: underbody, hackle legs, eyes, overbody.

Tier Comments: I found this pattern on the Internet, and it has worked for me as a Mangrove Tree Crab pattern. I fish it the same way as the Splat Crab, above. The pattern was originated by Charlie Craven, and can be modified to imitate any species of crab.

CHAPTER 3

Fiddler Crabs
Ocypodidae

Prey Type: Shoreline-associated crabs
Primary Habitats: Intertidal protected shorelines in mangroves, salt marshes, and flats
Geographic Range: Fiddler crabs occur in warm-temperate, subtropical, and tropical regions
Comments: Fiddler crabs live in burrows along protected shorelines, often at or near the high tide line. Many species feed on detritus that collects along the shoreline. Shallow, open bottom shorelines are favorite locations to use fiddler crab patterns. In the tropics and subtropics, black mangrove shorelines are prime habitats for using fiddler crab patterns. In warm-temperate marshes, shallow sloping, open bottom shorelines along marsh creeks, and open areas among marsh grass in the low marsh are prime habitats. Care should be taken to tie small fiddler crab flies.

Red drum are especially fond of fiddler crabs. In the salt marshes of the Carolinas, for example, fiddler crabs are among the red drum's most important diet items. In the southern part of the red drum's range, fiddler crabs aren't as important but are still popular with red drum in the shallows. Snook will also eat fiddler crabs when the opportunity presents itself. And during high spring tides in the tropics, bonefish will push onto flooded shorelines in search of fiddler crabs. I think the reason fiddler crabs have not shown up in the couple bonefish diet studies thus far conducted is that these studies have not sampled bonefish feeding in flooded mangrove shorelines.

Fiddler crab coloration can vary greatly (even within a species), depending on local conditions and time of year. It's a good practice to check local color varieties when tying new patterns.

Most of the photos below are of male fiddler crabs—only males have the enlarged claw, which is used in courtship and territorial display. In most cases, the enlarged claw is brighter or lighter in color than the carapace, and the fly patterns shown below take this into account.

Species: Burger's Fiddler Crab

Uca burgersi

Primary Habitats: Mud and sand bottoms along protected shorelines such as mangroves and creeks
Geographic Range: Southeast Florida, Caribbean
Size Range: to $1/2$ inch

Species: Caribbean Fiddler Crab

Uca rapax

Primary Habitats: Mud flats along mangrove shorelines and creeks
Geographic Range: South Florida, Caribbean
Size Range: to 1 inch

Species: Ive's Fiddler Crab

Uca speciosa

Primary Habitats: Muddy mangrove shorelines, near high tide line, brackish water
Geographic Range: Florida, northern Caribbean
Size Range: to $1/2$ inch

Species: Red-jointed Fiddler Crab

Uca minax

Primary Habitats: Muddy bottoms among marsh grasses (accessible to fish feeding in marshes near high tide)
Geographic Range: New England to northern Florida, northern Gulf of Mexico
Size Range: to 1 inch

Species: Mud Fiddler Crab

Uca pugnax

Primary Habitats: Muddy marsh surfaces
Geographic Range: New England to northeast Florida
Size Range: to $1/2$ inch

Species: Sand Fiddler Crab

Uca pugilator

Primary Habitats: Sheltered sandy shorelines
Geographic Range: New England to Florida
Size Range: to $1/2$ inch
Comment: This is probably the most common species throughout its range.

Species: Panacea Sand Fiddler Crab

Uca panacea

Primary Habitats: Sheltered sandy shorelines
Geographic Range: Gulf of Mexico
Size Range: to $1/2$ inch

Fiddler Crabs (Ocypodidae)

Species: Thayer's Sand Fiddler Crab

Uca thayeri

Primary Habitats: Muddy mangrove estuarine shorelines
Geographic Range: South Florida, Caribbean
Size Range: to ³/₄ inch

Species: Lavender Fiddler Crab

Uca vocator

Primary Habitats: Shaded muddy mangrove shorelines
Geographic Range: Caribbean
Size Range: to ¹/₂ inch

Species: Spined Fiddler Crab

Uca spinicarpa

Primary Habitats: Muddy mangrove shorelines, near high tide line, fresh water
Geographic Range: Northwestern Gulf of Mexico
Size Range: to ¹/₂ inch

Species: Long-wave Gulf Fiddler Crab

Uca longisignalis

Primary Habitats: Muddy marsh shorelines
Geographic Range: Gulf of Mexico
Size Range: to 1 inch

Species: Ghost Crab

Ocypode quadrata

Primary Habitats: Sandy beaches
Geographic Range: Mid-Atlantic and Gulf of Mexico through Caribbean
Size Range: to 2 inches
Comments: The burrows of ghost crabs are familiar sites along sandy beaches. Juvenile burrows are close to the high tide line, whereas adult burrows tend to be farther above the tide line. They drown if kept in water, but often run into the surf to wet their gills, grab something to eat (they're scavengers), or escape land-based predators. This is when gamefish have access to these prey.

FLIES

Prey Species: Fiddler Crab
Fly Pattern: No-look Fiddler
Fly Type: Impressionistic

TIER: AARON ADAMS

Hook: Mustad 34007, size 4
Tail: Brown marabou and gold Krystal Flash
Body: Tan Puglisi fiber, tied crossways on hook shank, trimmed to shape
Weight: Dumbbell eyes, gold
Thread: Danville flat waxed nylon, tan
Tying Tips: I tie this pattern in the style of Del Brown's Merkin, but I like to use Puglisi fibers for this pattern rather than yarn—the fly lasts longer and can be re-trimmed when it gets too bushy. Pull a small bunch of Puglisi fiber off the main bundle, and roll it between your thumb and fingers so that it looks like a stretch of yarn. Clip the rolled fiber bundle to appropriate lengths, and tie in as with a standard Merkin pattern (fiber bundles laid perpendicular to the hook shank, tied in with a

figure eight). The final step is to use scissors to trim the body flat—this can be repeated over time as the body becomes frayed with use.

Tier Comments: I use this pattern exclusively for red drum on open sand or mud bottom adjacent to black mangroves (black mangrove shorelines are often inhabited by fiddler crabs).

Prey Species: Fiddler Crab
Fly Pattern: Scrab
Fly Type: Imitation

TIER: GORDON CHURCHILL

Hook: Gamakatsu SC 15, size 1/0
Flash: Copper or whatever color Flashabou you have
Claws: Mallard flank feathers
Body: Good deer body hair for spinning
Legs: Rubber legs
Weight: Small dumbell eye
Thread: Flat waxed nylon, tan
Tying Tips: First tie the Flashabou and the mallard flank feathers in opposition, and then spin and stack one pack of deer hair. Next tie in the rubber legs, and spin and stack the second pack of deer hair. Tie in more rubber legs, spin and stack third pack of deer hair, and then trim the fly flat top and bottom; tie in the dumbbell, and go catch a fish.

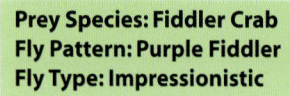

Prey Species: Fiddler Crab
Fly Pattern: Purple Fiddler
Fly Type: Impressionistic

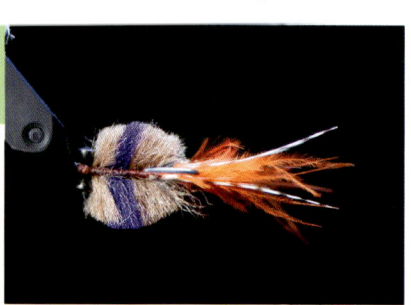

TIER: AARON ADAMS

Hook: Mustad 34007, size 4
Tail: Natural grizzly hackle tips outside orange marabou
Body: Tan and purple Puglisi fibers
Weight: Small dumbell eye
Thread: Danville flat waxed nylon, brown
Tier Comments: This is another pattern tied specifically for shallow shorelines of mangrove and salt marshes where fiddler crabs are most common.

Prey Species: Fiddler Crab
Fly Pattern: Hairball Fiddler
Fly Type: Impressionistic

TIER: AARON ADAMS

Hook: Mustad 34007, size 4
Body: Brown wool, spun and trimmed to shape
Tail: Light tan marabou over root beer Krystal Flash outside orange marabou
Weight: Small dumbell eye

Thread: Danville flat waxed nylon, brown
Tier Comments: Another impressionistic pattern tied specifically for shallow shorelines of mangrove and salt marshes where fiddler crabs are most common. The fly is so named because it looks a lot like something that a cat would throw up, but red drum like it.

Prey Species: Fiddler Crab
Fly Pattern: Fiddler Crab
Fly Type: Imitation

TIER: ANDRIJ HORODYSKY

Hook: Mustad 34007, size 6
Eyes: Burned 15-pound-test monofilament, colored olive with a permanent marker
Legs: Tan Vernille, tapered, knotted, stiffened with Zap-A-Gap, and colored with tan, orange, and olive permanent markers
Claws: Tan Aunt Lydia's sparkle yarn, knotted, stiffened with epoxy, and colored brown and red with permanent markers
Underbody: Lead tape, covered with E-Z Shape Sparkle Body
Body: Brown Aunt Lydia's sparkle yarn, tied in on the hook shank Merkin-style, packed tightly with a Brassie, and colored shades of brown, orange, and olive with permanent markers
Thread: Danville 6/0, tan

Tying Instructions
1. Taper the ends of three lengths of tan vernille with flame, and knot each one 1 centimeter from each end.
2. With hook point up, tie in the legs.
3. Knot two lengths of Aunt Lydia's sparkle yarn approximately 1 centimeter from the end, and tie in on either side of the midpoint of the hook shank.
4. Tie in 1-inch lengths of yarn Merkin-style along the entire hook shank, packing them tightly. Cut to the desired crab shape.
5. Press two layers of lead tape (cut smaller than the body) to the underside of the hook shank, and coat liberally with E-Z Shape Sparkle Body.
6. Shape the claws and apply clear 5-minute epoxy to stiffen. When dry, apply appropriate colors to body and legs.

Tier Comments: This realistic patterns represents fiddler crabs and, colored appropriately, mud crabs. It is designed to be fished passively in the currents around oyster reefs, pilings, bridges, and mangroves to mimic a dislodged crab. If an active retrieve is preferred, the legs should be tied with a livelier rubber or silicone material. Tied in all-cream coloration, this pattern can be fished in the surf to mimic ghost crabs.

CHAPTER 4

Spider Crabs
Majidae

Prey Type: Bottom-associated crabs
Primary Habitats: Open mud and sand bottoms, seagrass, rubble
Geographic Range: Most of the species covered here occur in tropical and subtropical regions. The southern spider crab occurs in warm-temperate and subtropical regions.
Comments: Most of the crab patterns shown in chapter 1 (Xanthidae, mud crabs) are just as applicable for spider crab patterns. Many of the species are similar in color and overall shape, and all are bottom-associated. In addition, an appropriately presented Del Brown's Merkin (tied in green and/or brown) is a good bet for imitating spider crabs.

Species: Southern Spider Crab

Libinia dubia

Primary Habitats: Open sand/mud bottom, seagrass
Geographic Range: New England to Florida, Gulf of Mexico
Size Range: to 4 inches
Comments: Similar species not shown (common spider crab, *Libinia emarginata*) occurs mostly in warm-temperate waters. Found on soft bottoms (mud, sand), the southern spider crab is a slow mover, so flies should be presented accordingly. These species grow rather large, but most individuals I have taken from fish stomachs (primarily red drum) are less than 2 inches. These species are prey for red drum in seagrass, on open bottom, and even along beaches.

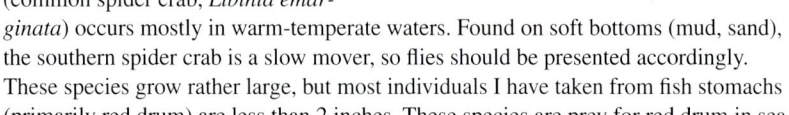

The next six species (genus *Mithrax* and *Pitho*) are favorites of bonefish and, to a lesser extent, permit and mutton snapper feeding in rubble and seagrass–rubble areas. In response to a predator, they usually scurry to the opposite side of the rubble to hide or wedge themselves into a crevice. This is important behavior to incorporate into fly design and presentation (i.e., sedentary rather than dynamic action—these crabs don't swim). The species eaten by bonefish and permit rarely grow larger than a nickel, and most individuals are smaller. Most species are found on hard structure (beachrock shoreline, rubble, coral) but seem to be most common as prey when this structure occurs in mixed habitats (e.g., rubble in seagrass). When fishing along beachrock shorelines or rubble zones in the tropics, *Mithrax* fly patterns are a good choice.

Species: Green Reef Crab

Mithrax sculptus

Primary Habitats: Rubble, seagrass mixed with rubble, reefs
Geographic Range: Florida, Bahamas, Caribbean
Size Range: to 1 inch

Species: Pitho Crab

Pitho mirabilis

Primary Habitats: Rubble, seagrass
Geographic Range: North Carolina to Florida, Gulf of Mexico, Caribbean
Size Range: to 1 inch

Species: Decorator Crab

Stenocionops furcata

Primary Habitats: Rubble, seagrass mixed with rubble, reefs
Geographic Range: Georgia to Florida, Caribbean
Size Range: to 6 inches, normally smaller

Spider Crabs (Majidae)

Species: Coral Spider Crab
Mithrax hispidus

Primary Habitats: Rubble, rocky bottom
Geographic Range: South Florida, Caribbean
Size Range: to 4 inches

Species: Gray Pitho Crab
Pitho aculeata

Primary Habitats: Rubble, seagrass
Geographic Range: North Carolina to Florida, Bahamas, Caribbean
Size Range: to 1 inch

Species: Tan Reef Crab
Mithrax coryphe

Primary Habitats: Rubble, seagrass, reefs
Geographic Range: Florida, Bahamas, Caribbean
Size Range: to 1 inch

FLIES

Prey Species: Crabs in the Genus *Mithrax*
Fly Pattern: Norman's Crab
Fly Type: Impressionistic

TIER: NORMAN SALESKI

Hook: Mustad 34007, size 4
Legs: Tan or olive Sili Legs
Claws: Natural or olive grizzly hackle tips
Body: Rabbit strip (tan or olive), tied in near hook eye

Weight: Small barbell or bead chain
Thread: Danville flat waxed nylon, white or olive
Tier Comments: Variations on this style have become popular bonefish patterns in recent years. I like to use the light-colored pattern on open sand bottom, and the dark pattern when fishing for bonefish in seagrass. It pays to add a weedguard to the darker pattern.

Prey Species: Spider Crab
Fly Pattern: Pom-pom Crab
Fly Type: Impressionistic

TIER: GLENN PITTARD

Hook: C47SD, size 1
Body: 10-millimeter pom-pom (available in craft stores)—color to suit
Legs: Rubber legs
Eyes: 25-pound-test Mason monofilament
Claws: Hackle, rabbit fur, or marabou

Tying Instructions

1. Crush barb and skewer pom-pom onto hook point, push around hook bend and forward to hook eye.
2. Start a thread base at the hook bend, and attach hackles for a wing, followed by two pieces of Mason monofilament with ends melted for eyes. Color them black with either paint or marker. Palmer a hackle over the thread wraps.
3. Dab some Zap-Gel or other glue over edge of thread wraps and hook shank; slide pom-pom back into place and allow glue to hold into place.
4. Once pom-pom is secure, legs can be attached. Using a sewing needle, thread a rubber leg through the pom-pom body, I like the look of three sets.
5. Body can be colored with permanent marker if preferred.

Prey Species: Mithrax Crab
Fly Pattern: Wool Spider Crab
Fly Type: Impressionistic

TIER: AARON ADAMS

Hook: Mustad 34007, size 4
Claws: Off-white neck hackle
Legs: Off-white rubber, barred with a black Sharpie
Body: Off-white wool
Weight: Dumbbell
Thread: Danville flat waxed nylon, white
Weedguard: 30-pound-test Ande monofilament (optional)
Tier Comments: This fly, and the olive version shown for mud crabs, works well in both seagrass and rubble areas where spider crabs and reef crabs are abundant. It works well on both bonefish and permit. The "blind," unweighted version (without eyes) is good for tailing red drum and bonefish in very shallow areas.

Prey Species: Mithrax Crab
Fly Pattern: Hackle Crab
Fly Type: Impressionistic

TIER: AARON ADAMS

Hook: Mustad 34007, size 6
Legs: Chartreuse and black Sili Legs or similar, tied in at the same spot, $1/3$ of the way down the hook shank from the hook eye
Body: Two or three olive grizzly hackles, tied in at the hook bend and palmered tightly to the hook eye
Eyes: Burned 30-pound-test monofilament, ends painted black with a Sharpie
Thread: Danville flat waxed nylon, olive
Weedguard: 20-pound-test Ande monofilament
Tier Comments: This fly resulted from a conversation I had with my friend Norman Saleski, who contributed the similar Norman's Crabs. The pattern is light, easy to cast, lands softly, and the hackle tips give the fly movement. This pattern works well in both seagrass and rubble areas where spider crabs and reef crabs are abundant. It can also be tied in tan or cream for light-colored bottoms.

CHAPTER 5

Porcelain Crabs
Porcellanidae

Prey Type: Bottom-associated crabs
Primary Habitats: Oyster or rocky bottoms
Geographic Range: Tropical, subtropical, and warm-temperate regions.
Comments: Porcelain crabs are more common around oyster bars and rocky bottoms than most people realize. They are usually rather secretive, flat-bodied, and colored similar to their surroundings. The two species shown here are similar in size and shape, differing in color. Porcelain crab flies need to be fished on the bottom, with short, rapid movements. Relative to other crab species in these habitats (e.g., mud crabs), porcelain crabs have long legs and claws in relation to their body size.

Species: Lined Porcelain Crab

Petrolisthes galathinus

Primary Habitats: Oyster bars and rocky bottom
Geographic Range: North Carolina through Caribbean
Size Range: to 3/4 inch

Species: Green Porcelain Crab

Petrolisthes armatus

Primary Habitats: Oyster bars and rocky bottom
Geographic Range: South Carolina through Caribbean, Gulf of Mexico
Size Range: to 3/4 inch

CHAPTER 6

Swimming Crabs
Portunidae

Prey Type: Bottom-associated crabs
Primary Habitats: Mangroves, seagrass, oyster bars, salt marshes, beaches, rubble, sand and mud flats
Geographic Range: Swimming crabs occur in warm-temperate, subtropical, and tropical regions
Comments: True to their name, swimming crabs use their paddlelike rear legs to swim in midwater and near the surface. They are on the menu of most coastal gamefish. Their high level of activity and diversity of behaviors (swimming, burrowing, and crawling across bottom) makes them good for imitating with flies and offers many ways to present the flies to gamefish. A reasonable amount of action can be given to these fly patterns, unlike flies to imitate mud and spider crabs, which must have little action. All of these crabs are similar in shape. Numerous other species of swimming crabs are present in coastal habitats, but those shown here are representative of the group. Among the most striking differences among the species is the coloration of their shells.

A common response of a crab that is swimming when a predator approaches is to dive for the bottom in search of cover—under a rock, under seagrass blades, or burying in sand or mud. Each of these strategies can be effective. Despite the predominance of dive-for-the-bottom strategies to escape predators, swimming crabs sometimes do try to outswim their predators, which may be why, sometimes, it is best to strip a crab imitation through midwater.

When really cornered, swimming crabs will flare their claws and face the predator in a last ditch effort to ward off the attack. Swimming crabs are fast and strong enough that predators can become wary when a swimming crab turns to face them. In most instances, predators will slurp in the crabs whole, but sometimes they will pick the crab apart. I once watched a group of four bonefish circle a large crab fly and pick at the rubber legs and hackle claws to dismember the crab before eating the body. Since that time, I tend to use smaller crab flies for bonefish.

Most gamefish eat swimming crabs. Bonefish, permit, and red drum have crusher plates in their mouths or throats that they use to crush the crab before swallowing it. Spotted seatrout, snook, and tarpon just swallow the crabs whole. How the gamefish eat the crabs should be considered when fishing with these patterns—you probably have more time to set the hook on the species that swallow the crabs whole, but you don't want to allow enough time for the crushers to crush the fly and spit it out.

Species: Blue Crab

Callinectes sapidus

Primary Habitats: Mangroves, seagrass, oyster bars, salt marshes, beaches, rubble, sand and mud flats

Geographic Range: New England to Florida, Gulf of Mexico, Caribbean

Size Range: to 6 inches or more, but juveniles are the primary prey for gamefish

Comments: The blue crab is perhaps the most common swimming crab species in the geographic coverage of this book. Although adult blue crabs are certainly eaten by gamefish, juveniles are most often targeted as prey. In some locations, phases of the moon can be used to target gamefish that are searching for soft-shelled blue crabs (blue crabs molt—grow new shells—numerous times throughout their lives). In lower Chesapeake Bay, for example, full moons in spring are good times to target spotted seatrout and striped bass searching for soft-shelled crabs in shallow grass beds.

Species: Lesser Blue Crab

Callinectes similis

Primary Habitats: seagrass beds, mud flats in high salinity areas

Geographic Range: U.S. Atlantic coast, northern and northwestern Gulf of Mexico

Size Range: to 6 inches or more, but juveniles are the primary prey for gamefish

Comments: The lesser blue crab is very similar in appearance to *Callinectes sapidus*, occurs in the same habitats and has a similar geographic range, but is probably limited to high-salinity areas (the blue crab can tolerate fresh water). The lesser blue crab is probably in highest abundance in the northern Gulf of Mexico. As with blue crabs, juveniles are the most likely target for gamefish.

Species: Red-Blue Crab

Callinectes bocourti

Primary Habitats: Shallow, mud or muddy-sand bottoms in estuaries

Geographic Range: Caribbean

Size Range: to 5 inches

Swimming Crabs (Portunidae)

Species: Ornate Blue Crab

Callinectes ornatus

Primary Habitats: seagrass beds, mud flats in high salinity areas
Geographic Range: Mid-Atlantic to Florida, southeastern Gulf of Mexico, Caribbean
Size Range: to 6 inches or more, but juveniles are the primary prey for gamefish

Species: Dana's Blue Crab

Callinectes danae

Primary Habitats: seagrass beds, mud flats in high salinity areas
Geographic Range: Caribbean
Size Range: to 6 inches or more, but juveniles are the primary prey for gamefish
Comments: This is a very common species in tropical estuarine and beach habitats.

Species: Iridescent Crab

Portunis gibbesii

Primary Habitats: Generally deeper sand bottoms, common swimming near the surface during spring and summer
Geographic Range: New England to Florida, Gulf of Mexico
Size Range: to $2^1/_2$ inches
Comments: Crabs in the *Portunus* genus are similar in appearance to the species in the genus *Callinectes*, but with more elongate legs and claws. This is the species of crab famously called pass crabs along the Gulf coast of Florida—a favorite of tarpon in early summer. Iridescent crabs normally live on the bottom, but during early summer on outgoing tides, they swim along the surface with the tide, presumably as part of the mating process. This is when they are most favored by tarpon. The bottom photo is the view fish feeding from below see when the crabs swim out of estuaries on the surface during ebbing tides.

CRABS

Species: Blotched Swimming Crab

Portunus spinimanus

Primary Habitats: Marine (full salinity) waters, sand and mud bottoms
Geographic Range: Mid-Atlantic and Gulf of Mexico to Brazil
Size Range: to 5 inches
Comments: This species has longer claws than its *Callinectes* counterparts, listed above, and usually has purplish tinges to its legs and claws. Like other *Portunus* species, it is a rather active crab and quick to flee when approached. Keep in mind, when tying crab flies that are designed to be fished in the upper portions of the water column, that gamefish will likely see the white underside of the crab.

Unidentified *Portunus* captured along a shallow sandy shoreline.

Species: Sargassum Swimming Crab

Portunus sayi

Primary Habitats: Floating sargassum mats
Geographic Range: New England to Florida, Gulf of Mexico, tropical Atlantic
Size Range: to 1 1/2 inches
Comments: Although this species really isn't a shallow-water coastal species, I list it here because coastal anglers do come across sargassum that has floated nearshore. In addition, this species may be found near other floating objects in coastal waters. Sargassum mats and other floating objects are also good habitats for tripletail (*Lobotes surinamensis*), which are found throughout the tropics and subtropics.

Swimming Crabs (Portunidae)

Species: Lady Crab

Ovalipes ocellatus

Primary Habitats: Sand bottom, often along beaches
Geographic Range: New England to northern Florida (a similar species—*Ovalipes floridanus*—occurs in the Gulf of Mexico)
Size Range: to 3 inches
Comments: The lady crab is limited to areas with full ocean salinity, generally open bottom habitats. This species is frequently eaten by red drum along beaches of the southeast coast, as well as by striped bass in the mid-Atlantic and farther north.

Species: Speckled Crab

Arenaeus cribrarius

Primary Habitats: Shallow sand bottom near shore and surf zone of beaches, entirely marine (not in estuarine habitats)
Geographic Range: New England to Florida, Gulf of Mexico to Brazil
Size Range: to 4 inches
Comments: At first glance, often confused with the lady crab. The speckled crab is also eaten by red drum and other beach-cruising gamefish. This is often the most abundant crab species along tropical and subtropical surf zones.

As swimming crabs swim sideways, the lead claw and nonswimming legs are tucked tight to the body, while the trailing claw trails straight out behind the crab. This should be a component of the fly design.

CRABS

FLIES

Prey Species: Iridescent Crab
Fly Pattern: Marabou Pass Crab
Fly Type: Impressionistic

TIER: AARON ADAMS

Hook: Owner 5115-121, size 2/0
Tail: One pair each of natural and purple grizzly hackle, splayed outward
Body: Palmered brown marabou
Thread: Danville flat waxed nylon, brown
Tier Comments: This is a standard pattern in somewhat nonstandard colors chosen for their similarity to the dominant colors of the iridescent crab that is eaten by tarpon during certain tides in spring along southwest Florida.

Prey Species: Iridescent Crab
Fly Pattern: Pass Crab Toad
Fly Type: Impressionistic

TIER: AARON ADAMS

Hook: Owner 5115-121, size 2/0
Tail: One pair each of natural and purple grizzly hackle, splayed outward
Wing: Palmered brown marabou
Body: Merkin-style body tied with tan Puglisi fibers
Thread: Danville flat waxed nylon, brown
Tier Comments: This has been a popular pattern in the Florida Keys and has recently gained popularity elsewhere. This is a somewhat nonstandard color combination, chosen for its similarity to the dominant colors of the iridescent crab that is eaten by tarpon during certain tides in spring along southwest Florida. The body is tied as in the Legless Merkin (see p. 34).

Swimming Crab Flies

Prey Species: Iridescent Crab
Fly Pattern: Floating Pass Crab
Fly Type: Imitation

TIER: GINGER ALLEN

Hook: Mustad 34007, size 3/0
Mouth: Lavender and purple marabou
Body: 3-millimeter craft foam, white belly, light brown back
Legs: Claret-colored neck hackle
Claws: Fuchsia black lace whiting hackle
Eyes: Epoxy coated large black glass bead on 60-pound-test mono stems
Thread: Gudebrod, red
Tier Comments: My husband and I had the great pleasure of fishing Captiva Pass with Aaron Adams one spring. We were waiting for the tidal flush of irridescent crabs upon which the tarpon feed. We found the crabs, but the tarpon were few and like wily coyotes. We could not get close enough to hook them. But Aaron and I had the opportunity to examine the crabs floating by and I tied this pattern up for next spring's crab flush. I found the bumpy brown foam in a craft store—you can also use smooth foam.

Prey Species: Swimming Crab
Fly Pattern: Del Brown's Merkin
Fly Type: Impressionistic

TIER: GLENN PITTARD

Hook: Mustad 34007, size 1, 1/0, or 2/0
Wing: Two pair tan grizzly hackles, splayed out; pearl or root beer Krystal Flash or thin Flashabou
Body: Tan and cream Puglisi fibers
Legs: White rubber hackle, ends painted red with permanent marker
Thread: Danville flat waxed nylon, chartreuse
Author Comments: This fly can be tied in a variety of colors to imitate numerous species of crabs, including swimming crabs, spider crabs, and mud crabs, with appropriate changes in presentation. Another coloring option is to tie with light-colored materials and color the top with permanent markers.

CRABS

Prey Species: Blue Crab
Fly Pattern: Dime Crab
Fly Type: Imitation

TIER: KEN BAY

Hook: Mustad 34007, size 1/0
Tail: Two pairs brown grizzly hackle (1 1/2 inches long), splayed outward at the bend of the hook, with Krystal Flash in the middle
Head: 1/50-ounce barbells behind hook eye
Body: Belly—white Velcro sticky back, trimmed to football shape. Stick on the upright hook; tie in with thread at each end.
Back: (the last step, see below)—on inverted hook, stick-on brown/tan felt shaped to match belly
Claws: Two Ultrasuede tan strips (1/8-inch wide, knotted for claws)
Legs: Four Ultrasuede strips (1/16 inch)
Eyes: Sewing pins with blackened heads
Thread: Tan nylon
Tying Tips: I put a drop of Krazy Glue on the knots and anchoring points of the legs. All parts are put in place on the sticky back of the Velcro, on the inverted hook. As the last step, cover all parts with FabriTac glue (available at craft stores), place the felt back on, and then squeeze the belly and back together with your fingers to complete sealing of the body. Vary this fly by gluing a feather on the back. I apply a yellow color to the bottom with a felt pen to discolor the stark white. Ultrasuede is used in marine/automotive upholstery.
Tier Comments: Back in the mid-1990s, I was able to get some Ultrasuede from Boyd Pfeiffer. This material is perfect for legs. I do not know of any fly that is more effective for sight-fishing for redfish than this pattern.

Prey Species: Blue Crab
Fly Pattern: Edible Blue Crab
Fly Type: Impressionistic

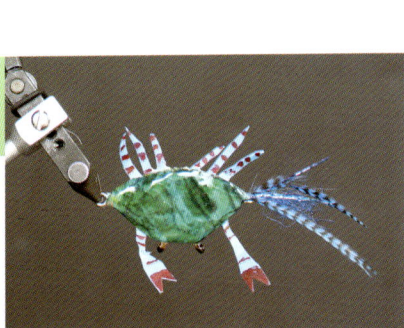

TIER: TOM BERRY

Hook: Eagle claw 066NF, size 4/0
Thread: Clear monofilament
Shell: Clear plastic cut to size, top colored with permanent blue marker
Underbody: Underside of shell filled with E-Z Shape Sparkle Body, white
Tail: Blue grizzly hackle and blue holographic Flashabou
Eyes: Burned 30-pound-test monofilament
Rattle: Small, inserted under shell, before sparkle body applied
Weight: .025-inch lead wire
Claws and Swimmers: Razor Foam

Swimming Crab Flies

Prey Species: Lady Crab
Fly Pattern: Merkin Spey
Fly Type: Impressionistic

TIER: DAVE SKOK

Hook: Tiemco TMC 811s, size 2/0
Eyes: Medium or large lead dumbbell eyes painted cream
Claws: Two pairs of pastel pink and orange saddle hackles, tied splayed
Body: Two white/cream and salmon whiting spey hackles wrapped, followed by alternating bands of cream and pale pink sparkle yarn, tied figure-eight style, trimmed to a crab shape
Legs: Three pairs of medium cream or tan Spanflex, marked with pink and black bands, square knotted between the bands of sparkle yarn
Thread: Flat waxed nylon, shell pink

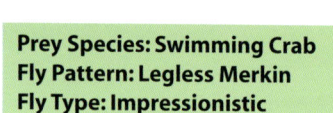

Prey Species: Swimming Crab
Fly Pattern: Legless Merkin
Fly Type: Impressionistic

TIER: AARON ADAMS

Hook: Mustad 34007, size 2 or 4
Tail: Tan craft fur, with bars marked with a black Sharpie
Body: Tan Puglisi fibers
Thread: Flat waxed nylon, chartreuse or pink

Tying Tips: I like to use Puglisi fibers for this pattern rather than yarn—the fly lasts longer and can be retrimmed when it gets too bushy. Pull a small bunch of Puglisi fiber off the main bundle, and roll it between your thumb and fingers so that it looks like a stretch of yarn. Clip the rolled fiber bundle to appropriate lengths, and tie in as with a standard Merkin pattern (fiber bundles laid perpendicular to the hook shank, tied in with a figure eight). The final step is to trim the body flat with scissors—this can be repeated over time as the body becomes frayed with use.

Tier Comments: This pattern is entirely focused on the silhouette of swimming crabs. As they swim sideways, the lead claw and nonswimming legs are tucked tight to the body, while the trailing claw trails straight out behind the crab. This pattern skips the addition of rubber legs in Del Brown's Merkin and is similar to the popular Kwan and to numerous similar patterns that used grizzly hackle rather than fly fur—it may also be known as a MerKwan.

Prey Species: Swimming Crab
Fly Pattern: Swimming Crab
Fly Type: Impressionistic

TIER: CHRIS DEAN

Hook: Mustad 34007, size 1/0
Claws: 1/8-inch-wide rubber bands, 1 inch long, tips colored red with a marker
Legs: Cream rubber, tips colored red with a marker
Eyes: Burnt monofilament (30-pound-test Mason); position the eyes between the hook and the Furry Foam and glue in place with 30-minute epoxy
Body: Olive Furry Foam, 3/4 inch wide; tie one end down at the hook bend, fold over, and tie the other end in at the hook eye
Belly: Cream Aunt Lydia's rug yarn cut up as if for dubbing, glued on to the bottom of the Furry Foam with clear silicon adhesive
Weight: Three strips of lead wire tied under the hook shank (not wrapped)
Thread: Flat waxed nylon, white
Tier Comments: I created this fly about three years ago. It works well for both permit and tripletail. The fly rides hook point down and is neutrally buoyant. The fly's buoyancy is controlled by the amount of lead wire tied into the fly. This pattern works well for cruising or floating fish.

Prey Species: Swimming Crab
Fly Pattern: Dean Permit Crab
Fly Type: Impressionistic

TIER: CHRIS DEAN

Hook: Mustad 34007, size 1/0
Eyes: Extra-large silver bead chain
Claws: A small bunch of deer hair spun behind the eyes and clipped short; then two brown neck hackles tied on each side, curving out
Body: Natural deer body hair spun and clipped flat on top and bottom, and clipped to crab shape
Thread: Flat waxed nylon, brown
Tying Tips: For the eyes, I use bead chain from ballyhoo trolling rigs. The deer hair step, when tying in the claws, forces the feathers to spread outward. Coat the center of the body with nail polish for added support. The fly should ride hook point down. To ensure this orientation, the bead chain eyes must be tied in well past the hook bend.
Tier Comments: I created this fly in 1980 to imitate a swimming crab. The fly sinks slowly (slightly heavier than neutrally buoyant) and works best on floating or cruising permit.

Prey Species: Swimming Crab
Fly Pattern: Fleeing Crab
Fly Type: Impressionistic

TIER: AARON ADAMS

Hook: Mustad 34007, size 2 to 1/0
Body: Cream Aunt Lydia's rug yarn, tied as for a Merkin
Legs: Eight off-white rubber legs, barred with brown permanent marker
Weight: Barbell eyes, size to match hook
Thread: Flat waxed nylon, pink
Tier Comments: This pattern, at least the way I tie it, is tied as a Del Brown's Merkin, with no claws and all legs trailing off the hook bend. It was originated by Lenny Moffo.

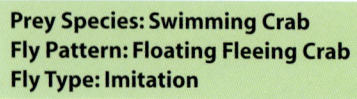

Prey Species: Swimming Crab
Fly Pattern: Floating Fleeing Crab
Fly Type: Imitation

TIER: AARON ADAMS

Hook: Mustad 34007, sizes 2 to 1/0
Weight: Bead chain, size to match hook, tied in near the hook bend
Claw: Tan grizzly hackle tips
Legs: Natural (off-white) round rubber legs, marked with black Sharpie
Underbody: White Neer Hair or Puglisi fibers, tied as for a Merkin
Carapace: White $1/8$-inch fly foam, cut to shape, top colored with an olive permanent marker
Swimmer: Tan grizzly hackle
Eyes: Burned 40-pound-test monofilament
Thread: Flat waxed nylon

Tying Instructions
1. Tie in the bead chain eyes.
2. Tie in the claw and legs at the hook bend.
3. Use the Neer Hair or Puglisi fiber to tie a Merkin-style body (see the Legless Merkin pattern for instructions).
4. Trim the Merkin body to shape.
5. With a pencil, trace the Merkin body on the foam.
6. Cut the foam to shape, and cut a slit in one end to pass around the hook shank bend.
7. Coat the top (hook point side) of the Merkin body with epoxy, place the eyes and hackles, and place the foam on top of all.
8. Squeeze the crab body lightly to make sure all parts stick together, and let sit to dry.

Tier Comments: This fly is a variation of Steve Huff's Fleeing Crab, modified to swim at or near the surface. This pattern definitely breaks my rule of a fast and simple tie, but I wanted a pattern that could be presented as a swimming crab—not one that drops to the bottom, but one that is trying to swim out of danger—near the surface. Fortunately, the fly is rather durable. The fly rides upper- to midwater, which is where swimming crabs often do their traveling.

Prey Species: Swimming Crab
Fly Pattern: Bonefish Joe
Fly Type: Impressionistic

TIER: LES FULCHER

Hook: Mustad 34007, size 2 or 4
Tail: Tuft of marabou or rabbit fur
Butt: Pink or orange Vernille
Claws: Cree hackles (one per side)
Collar: Spun deer hair
Weight: Lead or brass barbell, sized to hook
Head: Light tan chenille or rug yarn figure eight wrapped over barbell
Weedguard: 20-pound-test monofilament with burned ends to imply eyes

Prey Species: Swimming Crab
Fly Pattern: Merkin
Fly Type: Impressionistic

TIER: MARSHALL CUTCHIN

Hook: Partridge Sea Prince, size 1
Body: Aunt Lydia's craft yarn or similar yarn, alternating strands of tan and brown
Tail: Ginger saddle hackle
Legs: Small round tubber legs, with $1/4$-inch red tips made with indelible marker
Eyes: $7/32$-ounce (standard) or $3/16$-ounce (light) nickel/silver lead eyes
Thread: Danville flat waxed nylon, chartreuse
Tying Tips: I particularly like the hooking ability of recurved point on the Partridge Sea Prince; in fact, I've never had a fish fall off when using the hook. It's important to trim the yarn in a wedge shape back from the eyes to help keep the fly nose down and to keep it from wobbling—most commercial ties do not do this. Tie the rubber legs on

Swimming Crab Flies

with square knots to get them to extend more or less straight out from the hook shank, though I don't feel having the legs askew is anything other than cosmetic. Finally, I'm sparing with head cement, if I use it at all: Permit have a highly developed sense of smell, and I don't want to take any chances. The exact recipe can be duplicated in smaller sizes as a fantastic bonefish pattern. Tarpon also love to eat this fly.

Prey Species: Swimming Crab
Fly Pattern: Brown Recluse
Fly Type: Impressionistic

TIER: CRAIG SMOTHERS

Hook: Gamakatsu SC15-2H, size 3/0
Tail: Brown marabou surrounded by six to eight splayed brown dyed grizzly neck feathers, two strands of opal Mirage Accent
Collar: Asian red squirrel tail (difficult to find)
Thread: Brown Flymaster 6/0
Tier Comments: This fly was originated by Capt. Pat DeMarco.

Prey Species: Swimming Crab
Fly Pattern: Redfish Joe
Fly Type: Impressionistic

TIER: CRAIG SMOTHERS

Hook: Tiemco 811S, size 2
Tail: Tan calf tail between two splayed neck feathers, over which is two strands of root beer Krystal Flash, short orange ice chenille around the jam knot
Body: Spun natural deer body hair
Head/Eyes: $^6/_{32}$-ounce lead eyes painted white, overwrapped with tan chenille
Thread: Brown Flymaster+ 3/0
Tier Comments: This is the greatest redfish fly! Be sure to thoroughly pre-wet this fly so it sinks. Fish it slowly attached to a long leader. It works very well for blind casting in deeper water (2 to 4 feet). Due to the fact it's soft and chewy, the fish will hold onto it for that extra second for you to strip-strike them.

Prey Species: Swimming Crabs
Fly Pattern: Mike's Floating Crab
Fly Type: Imitation

TIER: MIKE MARSILI

Hook: 3/0 or 4/0 long shank, your brand of choice
Underbody: Chenille wrapped on shank to oval shape (higher in middle, tapered on ends)
Body: 1/8-inch fly foam, cut to crab shape
Claws, Legs: 1/8-inch fly foam, cut to length, segments made with thread wraps
Thread: Color and type of your choice—thread wraps are only for the underbody

Tying Instructions
1. Wrap chenille (color is unimportant) on hook shank, creating an oval shape, higher in the middle and tapered at each end.
2. Cut two pieces of foam to body shape—one for the top, one for the bottom.
3. Use Zap-A-Gap to glue the body foam onto the hook shank and chenille.
4. Use a razor to trim the body to shape and to taper the edges.
5. Cut strips of foam the length and width of the legs and claws.
6. For each leg or claw, secure the strip vertically in the vice, and use tying thread to create the segments. It's best to wrap a segment just above the vice jaws and then reposition the foam for the next segment.
7. After creating the segments for the claws, use scissors to cut the pincers, which should flare outward from the last segment.
8. Use Zap-A-Gap to attach the legs and claws to the underside of the body. To attach the legs, lay them flat along the body. The claws should be oriented vertically to the body before gluing.
9. Use a razor to trim the base of the legs so they taper to the body.

Tier Comments: This fly was designed for fishing to permit that are feeding on the surface, similar to trout feeding on dry flies. The fly can also be good for redfish or bonefish that are feeding in grass beds—attach a small split shot six inches or so up the tippet, and the fly will hover just above the grass blades. After tying them, field test the flies to see how they float. Every fly will be a little different, and you may need to use Zap-A-Gap to glue matchstick-style lead strips on the underside to make the fly float correctly.

CHAPTER 7

Mole Crabs
Hippidae

Prey Type: Bottom-associated crabs
Primary Habitats: Swash zone of exposed beaches
Geographic Range: Mole crabs occur in warm-temperate, subtropical, and tropical regions
Comments: Mole crabs live in the swash zone of sandy beaches (the area where the wash from waves rides up and falls down the beach), moving shoreward and seaward with the tide to stay in this zone. They use the energy from the waves to move up and down and along the beach, and they burrow in the sand when they want to stay put.

The key to fishing mole crab flies is to maintain a tight line while allowing the fly to move across the bottom with the waves. Mole crab flies can be fished blind (i.e., when you don't see gamefish), or while sight-fishing (my preference). Most gamefish feeding along sandy beaches will at least take a hard look at a well-presented mole crab fly, including permit, red drum, striped bass, snook, bonefish, and pompano.

All mole crab species listed here are nearly identical in size and appearance.

Species: Common Mole Crab

Emerita talpoida

Primary Habitats: Beach
Geographic Range: New England to Florida, Gulf of Mexico, Caribbean
Size Range: to $1^1/_2$ inches

CRABS

Species: Cuban Mole Crab

Hippa cubensis

Primary Habitats: Beach
Geographic Range: Florida, Bahamas, Caribbean, Gulf of Mexico
Size Range: to 1 1/2 inches

Species: Puerto Rican Mole Crab

Emerita portoricensis

Primary Habitats: Beach
Geographic Range: Florida, Bahamas, Caribbean, Gulf of Mexico
Size Range: to 1 1/2 inches

Species: Purple Surf Crab

Albunea gibbesii

Primary Habitats: Beach, sand flats
Geographic Range: North Carolina to Florida, Gulf of Mexico, Caribbean
Size Range: to 2 inches

Species: Webster's Mole Crab

Lepidopa websteri

Primary Habitats: Beach
Geographic Range: North Carolina to Florida, Gulf of Mexico
Size Range: to 2 inches

FLIES

Prey Species: Mole Crab
Fly Pattern: Woolly Mole
Fly Type: Imitation

TIER: AARON ADAMS

Hook: Mustad 34007, size 2 or 4
Legs: Tan Sili Legs
Eggs: Tuft of orange wool
Body: Tan and brown wool, spun or bunches tied crossways on hook shank, trimmed to shape
Weight: Brass dumbbell or brass cone slid onto hook shank prior to tying fly
Thread: Danville flat waxed nylon, tan
Tier Comments: This fly is best fished passively—allowed to roll around in the wash zone of the beach—but with enough tension on the line to feel a strike.

Prey Species: Common Mole Crab
Fly Pattern: Blind Crab
Fly Type: Imitation

TIER: DAVE SKOK

Hook: Mustad Signature C68S SS, size 1
Eyes: Small or medium lead dumbbell eyes (can be painted with tan, cream, or orange paint ahead of time)
Underside: Bleached elk
Legs: Cream Span-Flex (size M) barred pale pink and black
Underbody: Tan E-Z Bug and a ginger variant saddle hackle wrapped together to lead eyes—trim the hook point side after wrapping and apply head cement.
Carapace: Natural hare's ear magnum-cut zonker strip
Thread: Shell pink FW Nylon for dumbbells, tan 3/0 monocord for head

Prey Species: Mole Crab
Fly Pattern: Deerhair Mole Crab
Fly Type: Impressionistic

TIER: GINGER ALLEN

Hook: Mustad 34007, size 2
Tail: Tan marabou
Body: Three pairs of small bead chain eyes, spun natural brown deer hair
Thread: Gudebrod G, brown

Prey Species: Mole Crab
Fly Pattern: Marabou Mole Crab
Fly Type: Imitation

TIER: AARON ADAMS

Hook: Mustad 34007, size 4
Body: Orange and tan marabou, palmered, cut to shape
Weight: Medium brass barbell eyes
Thread: Danville flat waxed nylon, tan or brown

Tier Comments: An all-marabou pattern doesn't last very long, but the constant motion of the marabou in water makes this a good pattern for dead-drift fishing along beaches.

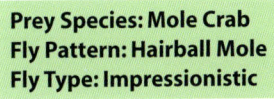

Prey Species: Mole Crab
Fly Pattern: Hairball Mole
Fly Type: Impressionistic

TIER: AARON ADAMS

Hook: Mustad 34007, size 4
Body: Palmered tan zonker strip
Legs: Tan rubber legs, colored with Sharpie pens
Weight: Medium brass barbell
Thread: Danville flat waxed nylon, pink

Tier Comments: It's ugly, but it's a fast and easy tie, and it works.

Mole Crab Flies

SECTION II
Shrimp

CHAPTER 8

Common Shrimp
Penaeidae

Prey Type: Bottom-associated Shrimp
Primary Habitats: Coastal bottom habitats, including seagrass, oyster bars, mangroves, marshes
Geographic Range: Common shrimp occur in warm-temperate, subtropical, and tropical regions
Comments: All three species of penaeid shrimp listed here are very similar in appearance. In general, the juveniles are found in the types of shallow estuarine habitats most frequently fished by fly anglers, so it is juvenile habitats that are listed for each species. The adults live in deeper water marine habitats.

Most gamefish eat common shrimp—they provide a lot of energy for their size, so they are tough for gamefish to pass up. A suitable shrimp imitation can be tied for any gamefish and be used successfully.

Species: Pink Shrimp

Farfantepenaeus duorarum

Primary Habitats: Seagrass, oyster bars, mangroves
Geographic Range: Warm-temperate and subtropical Atlantic and Gulf of Mexico
Size Range: Greater than 6 inches as adults, but generally smaller as juveniles in estuaries
Comments: Juvenile pink shrimp are the most common in seagrass beds—the other species prefer muddy estuarine bottoms. Young adults migrate out of estuarine juvenile habitats from spring through fall. Juvenile pink shrimp are high on the menus of red drum, snook, and bonefish. In the Florida Keys, the annual winter spawning migration of pink shrimp spurns a well-known feeding frenzy by tarpon and a host of other fish.

Photo on page 45: Shrimp are common residents of sand flats such as this one in the Bahamas.

Species: White Shrimp

Litopenaeus setiferus

Primary Habitats: Seagrass, oyster bars, marshes

Geographic Range: Warm-temperate Atlantic and Gulf of Mexico

Size Range: Greater than 6 inches as adults, but generally smaller as juveniles in estuaries

Comments: Juvenile white shrimp are common on muddy estuary bottoms, primarily in the warm-temperate region, and are most abundant in extensive estuarine marsh systems such as in South Carolina, Georgia, and the northern Gulf of Mexico. They prefer low salinity waters, 8–15 parts per thousand. If heavy rain causes salinities to drop in the tidal creeks, they will move farther down the estuary to higher salinity areas. In areas with a sufficient tidal range, such as the southeast coast, juvenile shrimp feed among the marsh grass in the low marsh at high tide, but they are forced into the creeks at low tide. In areas with less tidal range, such as the northern Gulf of Mexico, marsh edges are often a favorite habitat for white shrimp. They remain in the marsh creek habitats for the summer, when they move into larger creeks and rivers, and then offshore in late summer and fall.

Species: Brown Shrimp

Farfantepenaeus aztecus

Primary Habitats: Seagrass, oyster bars, mangroves
Geographic Range: Warm-temperate Atlantic and Gulf of Mexico
Size Range: Greater than 6 inches as adults, but generally smaller as juveniles in estuaries
Comments: Young adults move out of protected marsh areas in late spring and summer. In Texas, estuaries are brown shrimp nurseries in spring. Interestingly, despite their seasonal abundance in the northern Gulf of Mexico, brown shrimp are not especially abundant in red drum stomachs; red drum rank third, behind southern flounder and spotted seatrout, as the top gamefish predators of brown shrimp in estuarine habitats of the northern Gulf of Mexico.

FLIES

Prey Species: Pink Shrimp
Fly Pattern: Krystal Shrimp
Fly Type: Imitation

TIER: AARON ADAMS

Hook: Mustad 34011, size 4
Body: Brown chenille, overwrapped by tan grizzly hackle
Shellback: Root beer Krystal Flash
Eyes: Burned 30-pound-test monofilament
Thread: Danville flat waxed nylon, brown
Weedguard: 30-pound-test Ande monofilament

Tying Instructions
1. Tie in chenille and hackle at the hook bend.
2. Tie in eyes at hook bend.
3. Tie in flash with shorter ends extending over the hook bend, and bend long ends over the hook bend for the next steps.
4. Move thread to just behind hook eye.
5. Wrap chenille to thread location, and tie in.
6. Palmer hackle to thread location, and tie in.
7. Move thread back approximately a third of the way toward the hook bend along hook shank.
8. Fold long ends of flash toward hook eye to the thread location, and take a few thread wraps.
9. Move thread a third of the distance back toward hook eye, lay Flash, and wrap thread a few times.
10. Repeat step 9 one more time.
11. Tie in Flash just behind the hook eye, leaving room for a weedguard.
12. Tie in the weedguard and whip-finish.

Tier Comments: This fly has done well on red drum tailing in seagrass beds.

Prey Species: Pink Shrimp
Fly Pattern: Fur Shrimp
Fly Type: Imitation

TIER: AARON ADAMS

Hook: Mustad 34011, size 4
Body: Brown chenille, overwrapped by tan grizzly hackle
Shellback: Tan fly fur or Kinky Fiber
Eyes: Burned 30-pound-test monofilament
Thread: Danville flat waxed nylon, brown
Weedguard: 30-pound-test Ande monofilament

Tier Comments: This fly is tied identically to the Krystal Shrimp (above) but is less flashy for clear water or spooky fish.

Prey Species: Common Shrimp
Fly Pattern: KB Indian River Shrimp
Fly Type: Imitation

TIER: KEN BAY

Hook: Mustad 34011, size 2
Mouth: 1/2-inch calf tail
Antennae: Two brown Krystal Flash strands (stain pearl with a brown felt marker)
Eyes: Melted monofilament, ends blackened
Body: Pearl estaz stained with marker #PM154 Prismacolor Mineral Orange, overstained with marker #PM90 Walnut for copper color
Legs: Palmered brown grizzly hackle
Shellback: White Super Hair or equivalent, stained with marker #PM154 and #PM90 marker, as for body
Ribbing: 20-pound-test monofilament, stained brown with marker
Overlay: Clear silicone with copper Krystal Flash embedded
Thread: White
Tying Tips: Optional eyes are plastic flower stamens (aka Spray Pips in craft stores) coated with epoxy, painted with copper opaque paint marker (by DecoColor). Color half the eye tip with a black Sharpie.
Tier Comments: This pattern has been quite a success since 1998 when it appeared in *Saltwater Fly Fishing*. It is an adaptation of Popovics's Ultra Shrimp, with major changes such as a bent hook for a different profile and a silicone shell back. I make this pattern in many colors to match local variations.

Prey Species: Common Shrimp
Fly Pattern: Leftover Shrimp
Fly Type: Imitation

TIER: RON WINN

Hook: Mustad 34007, size 1/0
Head: White bucktail topped with natural bucktail, under palmered brown and white hackle butt ends
Legs: Tan rubber legs
Body: Gold ice chenille
Topping: Poly bag (4 millimeter) ribbed with monofilament
Eyes: Monofilament with plastic beads epoxied to ends
Thread: Fine monofilament

Common Shrimp Flies

Prey Species: Pink Shrimp
Fly Pattern: Pink Spey Shrimp
Fly Type: Impressionistic

TIER: GINGER ALLEN

Hook: Mustad 34007, size 1
Body/Horn: Palmered shrimp color spey feather, topped with flat poly twine and head cement (optional underbody of wrapped lead wire)
Eyes: 20-pound-test burnt mono
Front Legs: Two splayed shrimp pink spey feathers
Thread: Clear mono

Prey Species: Brown Shrimp
Fly Pattern: Tarpon Brown Shrimp Streamer
Fly Type: Impressionistic

TIER: GINGER ALLEN

Hook: Mustad 34007, size 2/0
Tail: Brown deer hair, six blonde neck hackle splayed out, gold flash
Collar: Eastern fox squirrel or gray squirrel
Body: White thread built up; then wrapped with pearl metallic thread and coated lightly with epoxy
Thread: Gudebrod G, white
Tier Comments: This fly was originated by Stu Apte.

Prey Species: Common Shrimp
Fly Pattern: DH Shrimp
Fly Type: Impressionistic

TIER: DOUG HEDGES

Hook: Mustad 34007, size 2
Tail: Brown/black barred grizzly hen hackles with brown Sili Legs
Eyes: Colored burnt mono
Body: Natural deer body hair
Head: Brown mohair
Weight: Extra small dumbbell eyes
Thread: Danville flat waxed nylon, brown
Weedguard: 17-pound-test Hard Mason doubled monofilament

Prey Species: Brown Shrimp
Fly Pattern: Brown Gulf Shrimp
Fly Type: Impressionistic

TIER: TOM BERRY

Hook: Eagle Claw 066NF, size 2/0
Antennae: Orange saltwater Krystal Flash
Throat: Tan or light brown Super Hair
Front Legs: Pearlescent Flashabou accent
Back Legs: Opal root beer estaz
Underbody: Tan ultra-chenille
Overbody: Clear plastic, cut to shape, colored with permanent markers
Eyes: $9/32$-inch molded eyes
Weight: .025-inch lead wire
Thread: Clear monofilament
Coating: Clear epoxy over the underbody

Prey Species: Common Shrimp
Fly Pattern: Bendback Gurgler
Fly Type: Impressionistic

TIER: AARON ADAMS

Hook: Mustad 34011, size 4
Tail: Brown bucktail, over which is root beer Flashabou
Body: Palmered tan grizzly hackle
Back: $1/8$-inch tan fly foam
Thread: Danville flat waxed nylon, brown

Tier Comments: This is the standard Gartside Gurgler tied on a long shank hook with the hook bent back so the fly rides hook point up. This makes the fly weedless, which is essential for using this fly in areas with thick seagrass growing to the water surface. This pattern is great for fishing to tailing red drum in thick seagrass. It is tied in brown and tan to imitate juvenile shrimp common to seagrass beds.

There are days when red drum will follow the Gurgler, only to turn away at the last minute. When this behavior occurs, I like to tie an unweighted shrimp pattern (a Krystal Shrimp works well) as a trailer/dropper. Tie the shrimp to the hook bend of the Gurgler with 15-pound leader, about 6 inches behind the Gurgler.

Prey Species: Common Shrimp
Fly Pattern: Clouser Minnow, tan or brown
Fly Type: Impressionistic

TIER: AARON ADAMS

Hook: Mustad 34007, size 1
Underwing: White bucktail
Overwing: Tan or brown bucktail over root beer Krystal Flash
Weight: Brass dumbbells, medium
Thread: Danville flat waxed nylon, brown or pink
Tier Comments: This standard pattern is perhaps one of the most-used patterns in saltwater fly fishing. I tend to use this color combination when fishing in areas with any of the shrimp species (common shrimp, snapping shrimp, ghost shrimp), generally on open bottom, but it can be used in many different situations. A brown-and-white version resulted in my first bonefish on fly.

Prey Species: Common Shrimp
Fly Pattern: Cactus Clouser
Fly Type: Impressionistic

TIER: AARON ADAMS

Hook: Mustad 34007, size 1
Body: Root beer cactus chenille
Wing: Tan bucktail, root beer Krystal Flash
Weight: Brass dumbbells, medium
Thread: Danville flat waxed nylon, brown
Tier Comments: This is a good pattern for red drum. When used in areas with seagrass, a weedguard should be added.

Prey Species: Common Shrimp
Fly Pattern: Tarpon Shrimp
Fly Type: Impressionistic

TIER: AARON ADAMS

Hook: Mustad 34007, size 3
Underwing: Light brown marabou
Overwing: Brown cree hackle, one each side, splayed outward
Underbody: Tan chenille
Overbody: Palmered brown grizzly hackle
Thread: Danville flat waxed nylon, brown

Tier Comments: This fly does well in backcountry areas where tarpon often feed on shrimp, and it can be dead-drifted in currents when tarpon are feeding on migrating shrimp.

Prey Species: Common Shrimp
Fly Pattern: Ugly Shrimp
Fly Type: Impressionistic

TIER: AARON ADAMS

Hook: Mustad 34011, size 2
Wing: Tan marabou over root beer Krystal Flash
Eyes: Burned 30-pound-test monofilament
Body: Palmered natural grizzly hackle, densely wrapped
Weedguard: 30-pound-test Ande monofilament
Thread: Danville flat waxed nylon, brown
Tier Comments: This fly is specifically for spooky tailing red drum in seagrass beds. It lands lightly and hovers midwater, so it doesn't get lost among the seagrass blades. Silver bead chain eyes can be added near the hook eye to get the fly down faster, if desired.

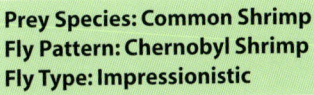

Prey Species: Common Shrimp
Fly Pattern: Chernobyl Shrimp
Fly Type: Impressionistic

TIER: CHRIS DEAN

Hook: Mustad 34007, size 1
Tail: Light brown craft fur barred with a black marker, orange Krystal Flash on each side
Collar: Natural deer body hair
Body: Natural deer body hair clipped short
Hackle: Natural brownish hackle palmered through body, clipped off at bottom
Eyes: Large gold bead chain
Weedguard: 20-pound-test Mason, double beard
Thread: Flat waxed nylon, white
Tier Comments: I started tying this fly about four years ago. It's a variation of Tim Borski's Chernobyl Crab. It's another shrimp imitation for redfish at Flamingo.

Prey Species: Common Shrimp
Fly Pattern: Dean Redfish Fly
Fly Type: Impressionistic

TIER: CHRIS DEAN

Hook: Mustad 34007, size 2/0 (use needle-nose pliers to bend the hook into a bendback position)
Body: Silver Mylar overwrapped with yellow monofilament (20–40 pound test)
Wing: Saddle or neck hackles 2^1/$_2$ inches long, tied divided wing–style (yellow inside grizzly inside orange), one set on each side
Collar: Orange-dyed brown bucktail (back side of orange-dyed bucktail) covering the sides and top of the wing
Head: Painted fluorescent orange, coated with clear nail polish
Thread: Flat waxed nylon, orange
Tier Comments: I developed this fly in the early 1980s, trying to make a weedless redfish fly for the Flamingo area. After trying several weedless methods, I changed to the bendback style, which works great. The fly is a shrimp imitation with bright colors for visibility—for both me and the redfish. I think it's important to see where the fly is relative to the fish's position.

Prey Species: Common Shrimp
Fly Pattern: Leech Shrimp
Fly Type: Impressionistic

TIER: CHRIS HUMPHREY

Hook: Owner Mosquito, sizes 6 to 4/0
Wing: Copper Krystal Flash (two strands), furnace neck hackles, sparse brown bucktail
Legs: Palmered grizzly hackle
Body: Tan leech yarn
Eyes: Nylon
Thread: Flat waxed nylon, gray

Tying Instructions

1. Tie in a small clump of bucktail and then two strands of Krystal Flash. Make a few wraps of thread under the bucktail to make it angle up slightly. This will serve as the "head" long after the feathers are gone.
2. Tie in two thin neck hackles.
3. Tie in a webby grizzly hackle, leech yarn, and the nylon eyes.
4. Make several figure-eight wraps around the eyes and then palmer the leech yarn to behind the hook eye and secure with thread wraps.
5. Palmer the grizzly hackle and secure at the hook eye.
6. Trim the hackle short on the top and sides.
7. Tease out some of the leech yarn around the hook bend.

Tier Comments: This fly is deadly when shrimp are the main prey in the area. It can be drifted in the current or cast to a specific target. Lighter color combinations can be fished around lights at night. This is my go-to fly when rolling tarpon are around. I've caught snook, tarpon, bonefish, spotted seatrout, redfish, snapper, grouper, and permit with this fly. It works extremely well in current.

Prey Species: Common Shrimp
Fly Pattern: Buz's Shrimp
Fly Type: Impressionistic

TIER: BUZ FENDER

Hook: Mustad Signature S71sss or Mustad 34007, sizes 2, 4
Body: Tan estaz (can also be tied in peach, chartreuse, white)
Wing: Tan craft fur (or color to match body)
Antennae: Black or peacock green Krystal Flash
Legs: Sili Legs, amber fleck or silver pearl, with red tips
Weight: $1/50$- or $1/100$-ounce dumbbell
Thread: Danville flat waxed nylon, color to match body
Weedguard: 20-pound-test Mason monofilament (can burn ends to make eyes)
Optional: Krystal Flash (color to match body) over the weedguard
Tier Comments: I like to use this pattern on shallow flats for redfish and for tailing redfish. If the turtle grass is especially thick, I use a weightless version. Tie in this sequence: antenna, craft fur, estaz, Sili Legs, palmer estaz, weedguard, and weedguard cover.

Prey Species: Common Shrimp
Fly Pattern: Coker Smoker
 (originated by Fitz Coker)
Fly Type: Impressionistic

TIER: AARON ADAMS

Hook: Owner 5311-121, size 2/0
Wing: Two tan grizzly and one yellow grizzly hackle on each side, splayed out
Collar: Light tan marabou, palmered around hook shank
Front collar: Palmered tan grizzly hackle
Thread: Flat waxed nylon, tan
Tier Comments: I've found this fly, originated by Fitz Coker, to be productive in backcountry conditions with clear water, where tarpon come across subadult and juvenile shrimp. I like to use longer marabou for the collar than what is called for in the original pattern.

Common Shrimp Flies 55

Prey Species: Common Shrimp
Fly Pattern: Bunny Shrimp
Fly Type: Impressionistic

TIER: AARON ADAMS

Hook: Owner 5311-121, size 2/0
Tail: Tan zonker strip
Stabilizer: 30-pound-test monofilament pierced through zonker skin, halfway along tail, tied in at hook shank
Collar: Tan zonker strip palmered around hook shank
Thread: Flat waxed nylon, tan
Tier Comments: This is a shrimp-colored version of the standard Tarpon Bunny.

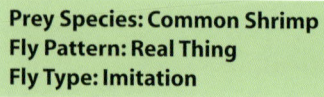

Prey Species: Common Shrimp
Fly Pattern: Real Thing
Fly Type: Imitation

TIER: AARON ADAMS

Hook: Mustad 34007, size 2
Forelegs: Tan marabou tips, over pearl Krystal Flash
Eyes: Burned 30-pound-test monofilament, ends blackened with Sharpie
Body: Medium tan chenille
Legs: Palmered light brown hackle
Shellback: Tan Kinky Fiber, tied in at the hook eye, attached to the body with Softex, applied liberally as a shellback
Antennae: Root beer Krystal Flash
Thread: Flat waxed nylon, white
Weedguard: 20-pound-test monofilament
Tier Comments: Small juvenile common shrimp are very similar in appearance to grass shrimp. In fact, a couple grass shrimp species not shown here reach lengths large enough to be mistaken for small common shrimp. In addition, their behaviors are similar enough that many of the patterns (appropriately sized) are suitable for either group.

Prey Species: Common Shrimp
Fly Pattern: Hophead
Fly Type: Impressionistic

TIER: STEVE VENINI

Hook: Mustad 34007, size 2
Tail: Pearl Krystal Flash over Puglisi fiber, cream, barred with orange and brown Sharpie markers
Forelegs: Black holographic Flashabou over tan Sili Legs

SHRIMP

Eyes: Puglisi crab and shrimp eyes
Underbody: Lead wire wrapped around $1/2$ of hook shank
Wing: Tan fox fur
Thread: Flat waxed nylon, brown
Weedguard: 20-pound-test monofilament

Tying Instructions
1. After tying in the tail, forelegs, and eyes, the overbody and wing are tied with the same clump of fox fur.
2. Tie in the clump of fox fur backward near the hook bend—the butt ends pointing toward the hook bend and the tips pointing toward the hook eye.
3. Move the thread forward, and secure the middle portion of the fox fur just behind the hook eye.
4. Whip-finish and tie off. Reattach the thread near the hook bend, lay the fox fur backward over the eyes, and wrap with thread to secure in place.
5. Whip-finish and trim the thread.
6. Reattach the thread at the hook eye, tie in the weedguard, whip-finish, and trim.

Prey Species: Common Shrimp
Fly Pattern: Ropp's Redfish Bendback
Fly Type: Impressionistic

TIER: CRAIG SMOTHERS

Hook: Mustad 34011, size 4
Tail: Brown marabou with two strands of root beer Krystal Flash
Body: Brown Aunt Lydia's rug yarn, palmered barred ginger saddle feather
Eyes: $5/32$-ounce gold brass eyes
Wing: Brown center hair from an orange or yellow dyed bucktail, two to three strands of root beer Krystal Flash
Thread: Flymaster 3/0, brown

Tying Tips: When building the body, palmer the feather between wraps of the rug yarn. This will dramatically improve its durability. When tying the wing in, allow the hair to extend about $1/4$ inch past the hook eye. Then fold this hair back and overwrap it with thread. This lump of hair acts as an improved weedguard (not fish-guard).

Tier Comments: When fishing this fly, try using a 6-pound-test sinking shooting head with a 12-foot leader. A long leader on a sinking head goes against all conventions but puts the head directly along the bottom while allowing the fly to ride right along the tops of the seagrass. This is deadly effective when blind-casting in deeper (3 to 4 foot) turtle grass. This fly was originated by John Ropp.

Prey Species: Common Shrimp
Fly Pattern: Sugarman Shrimp
Fly Type: Impressionistic

TIER: CRAIG SMOTHERS

Hook: Mustad 34007, sizes 1 to 4
Tail: Palmered golden pheasant red body feather
Body: Chartreuse Uni Stretch thread, small palmered cree neck feather
Eyes: $^4/_{32}$-ounce gold brass Dazl Eye
Wing: Tan calf tail, two strands of pearl Flashabou
Thread: Flymaster 6/0, chartreuse
Tier Comments: Stan Sugarman used this for everything from bonefish to permit to redfish—sized and weighted accordingly.

Prey Species: Common Shrimp
Fly Pattern: Watch It Wiggle Bendback
Fly Type: Impressionistic

TIER: CRAIG SMOTHERS

Hook: Mustad 34011, size 1
Tail: Olive-dyed Arctic fox body hair, three strands of olive or peacock Krystal Flash
Body: Olive New Age chenille, three round olive glittered silicone legs
Eyes: $^5/_{32}$-ounce gold brass Dazl Eyes
Wing: Olive-dyed Arctic fox body hair, three strands of olive or peacock Krystal Flash on each side
Thread: Flymaster+ 3/0, olive
Tier Comments: Arctic fox body hair is the new-age marabou. It comes in a myriad of colors, breathes like marabou, and is substantially tougher. I often substitute it for marabou. This pattern is equally representative of various shrimp.

CHAPTER 9

Ghost and Mud Shrimp
Callianassidae and Thalassinidae

Prey Type: Bottom-associated shrimp
Primary Habitats: Shallow coastal open bottom habitats
Geographic Range: Ghost shrimp occur in warm-temperate, subtropical, and tropical regions
Comments: Ghost and mud shrimp live in double-ended burrows in the bottom of intertidal and shallow subtidal areas. They mostly feed by filtering particles that enter the burrow on currents created by movements of the shrimp's legs. They emerge from their burrows on occasion to feed on detritus and for territory defense and mating. Many of the sand and mud mounds on the flats are made by these species. When excavated from their burrows, their escape mechanism is to burrow back into the bottom as quickly as possible.

These species are all very similar in appearance, with species identification based on micro-characteristics such as presence/absence of a tooth on the claw and number of lobes on the telson (tail), so only one photograph is shown here for reference. All species listed here are pale in color.

Ghost and mud shrimp do not appear to be abundant in any gamefish diet (based on scientific studies), but gamefish enthusiastically eat them when the opportunity arises. In fact, they are popular bait for anglers in many warm-temperate locations. When presented with a ghost or mud shrimp, most gamefish eat it without hesitation. These may be one of the species being pursued by bonefish jetting water into soft bottom in search of prey.

GHOST SHRIMP

Species: West Indian Ghost Shrimp
Callianassa major

Primary Habitats: Mud and sand bottom
Geographic Range: North Carolina to Florida, Gulf of Mexico, Caribbean
Size Range: to $3^3/4$ inches

Species: Atlantic Ghost Shrimp

Callianassa atlantica

Primary Habitats: Mud and sand bottom
Geographic Range: New England to Florida
Size Range: to 3$^{1}/_{4}$ inches

Species: Trilobed Ghost Shrimp

Callianassa trilobata

Primary Habitats: Mud and sand bottom
Geographic Range: Gulf of Mexico
Size Range: to 3$^{1}/_{4}$ inches

MUD SHRIMP

Species: Mud Shrimp

Upogebia affinis

Primary Habitats: Mud and sand bottom
Geographic Range: New England to Florida, Gulf of Mexico, Caribbean
Size Range: to 4 inches

FLIES

Prey Species: Ghost Shrimp
Fly Pattern: Big Ugly
Fly Type: Impressionistic

TIER: AARON ADAMS

Hook: Mustad 34007, size 2 or 4
Tail: Tan fly fur over brown grizzly hackle; mark bars on the fly fur with permanent marker
Body: Root beer cactus chenille tied in at the hook bend, palmered to behind the hook eye
Wing: Tan fly fur or angora wool
Weight: Medium barbells, eyes painted on
Thread: Danville flat waxed nylon, pink
Tier Comments: I came up with this pattern before a research trip to Andros, Bahamas. A guide on Andros, Phillip Rolle, who was helping with the research, took one look at the fly and proclaimed it the Big Ugly. But by the time the week was done, Phillip was using the fly too.

Prey Species: Ghost Shrimp
Fly Pattern: Sparkle Ugly
Fly Type: Impressionistic

TIER: AARON ADAMS

Hook: Mustad 34007, size 2
Wing: Tan fly fur, bars marked with a brown permanent marker; tuft of cream marabou
Body: Root beer cactus chenille tied in at the hook bend, palmered to behind the hook eye
Legs: Light brown grizzly hackle, tied in at the hook bend, palmered to the hook eye, trimmed on top
Eyes: Burned 30-pound-test monofilament, ends painted black with permanent marker
Thread: Danville flat waxed nylon, pink
Weight: Medium barbells, eyes painted on

CHAPTER 10

Mantis Shrimp
Squillidae

Prey Type: Bottom-associated shrimp
Primary Habitats: Shallow coastal habitats including seagrass beds, mangroves, sand and mud bottoms, oyster bars, coral rubble
Geographic Range: Mantis shrimp occur in subtropical and tropical regions
Comments: There are dozens of mantis shrimp species in the geographic area covered by this book. Listed here are what I believe to be the most common species in habitats frequented by anglers. Each of these species is able to change color to match their surroundings. They can't change color quickly, as can some fish, but can take on a new color when they molt (grow a new shell).

The forward appendages of mantis shrimp are used to capture prey and are dangerous enough to warrant caution if handled. Some mantis shrimp have sharp forward appendages that they use to slice prey. Others have what amount to club-ends that they use to bludgeon prey.

Some species lay in wait at their burrow entrances and ambush passing prey. Other species move around in search of prey. When they are approached by a predator, they usually turn to face the predator and walk or swim backwards. On occasion they will snap their tails to jet backwards toward cover.

Permit, bonefish, and red drum are the main gamefish predators of mantis shrimp, but other gamefish will probably eat them if given the chance.

Species: Rock Mantis Shrimp

Gonodactylus oerstedii

Primary Habitats: Rubble, open sand
Geographic Range: North Carolina to Florida, Gulf of Mexico, Caribbean
Size Range: to 4 inches
Comments: This species can vary in coloration, from dark green or black to cream or bright green. It is common in rubble areas and beachrock shorelines of the tropics.

Species: Common Mantis Shrimp

Squilla empusa

Primary Habitats: Rubble, oyster bars, open sand, mud bottom
Geographic Range: Mid-Atlantic to Florida, Gulf of Mexico, Caribbean
Size Range: to 8 inches, usually smaller
Comments: These shrimp live in U-shaped burrows in muddy bottoms but can be found swimming in midwater over seagrass beds and near the surface at night. This species can also vary in coloration, including dark and light green, tan, and the orange seen here.

Species: Golden Mantis Shrimp

Pseudosquilla ciliata

Primary Habitats: Rubble, open sand
Geographic Range: North Carolina to Florida, Gulf of Mexico, Caribbean
Size Range: to 3 inches
Comments: Like the first two species, individuals tend to be colored to match their surroundings, so they may be tan in rubble and sandy bottoms and green in seagrass. This species is common throughout the tropics as well as in subropical areas. And similar to the common mantis shrimp, the golden mantis can be found swimming in midwater over seagrass areas.

Mantis Shrimp (Squillidae)

FLIES

Prey Species: Green Mantis Shrimp
Fly Pattern: Green Mantis Shrimp
Fly Type: Imitation

TIER: KEN BAY

Hook: Mustad 34011, 1/0 or larger, bend back $1/2$ inch behind eye, 1-inch flat lead strip at rear of hook
Antennae: Peccary quills
Eyes: Melted monofilament, ends painted chartreuse
Claws: Tan Ultrasuede on inverted hook, pink edges at tips
Body: Olive estaz
Legs: Brown grizzly hackle
Shellback: Lime-green Fishair, darkened with green felt marker (#PM166 Prismacolor), coated with two to three applications of Softex
Tier Comments: While this is pretty much a takeoff of Carl Richards's construction, I think I made it easier to tie and created prominent claws to attract fish. When I showed some flies of different color shades to bait fishermen at the local tackle shop, the consensus was that the model shown here was closest to the natural, and this fly met with their approval—the tannish claws, darkened body, and green coloration they saw on the naturals.

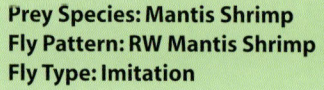

Prey Species: Mantis Shrimp
Fly Pattern: RW Mantis Shrimp
Fly Type: Imitation

TIER: RON WINN

Hook: Mustad 34011, size 4
Body: Olive crystal chenille
Antennae: Krystal Flash, fine rubber strands
Eyes: Monofilament epoxied to plastic beads
Shellback: Poly bag (4 millimeter)
Ribbing: 6-pound-test monofilament
Weight: Lead wire wrapped around hook shank
Thread: Fine monofilament
Weedguard: Larva lace

Prey Species: Mantis Shrimp
Fly Pattern: Bunny Mantis
Fly Type: Impressionistic

TIER: AARON ADAMS

Hook: Mustad 34007, size 2 or 4
Wing: Tan fly fur; mark bars on the fly fur with permanent marker
Body: Pink thread over hook shank; tan grizzly hackle tied in at the hook bend and palmered to the hook eye; tan zonker strip, tied in at the hook bend and behind the hook eye
Weight: Medium brass barbells
Thread: Danville flat waxed nylon, pink
Tier Comments: This is a variation of the Big Ugly (see page 60), but with the rabbit strip and hackle, the fly appears active even when not being stripped. This is a good fly for fish that are spooky toward a stripped fly.

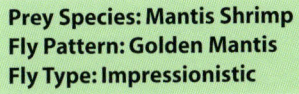

Prey Species: Mantis Shrimp
Fly Pattern: Golden Mantis
Fly Type: Impressionistic

TIER: AARON ADAMS

Hook: Mustad 34007, size 2 or 4
Body: Light yellow chenille under palmered brown grizzly hackle
Wing: Tan Fishair
Legs: Tan Sili Legs
Eyes: Burned 20-pound-test monofilament
Weight: Medium barbells
Thread: Danville flat waxed nylon, yellow
Tier Comments: I first tied and used this pattern in Belize for permit, and they reacted well to this and an olive version. A green version can be tied for areas with mixed coral rubble and seagrass on Caribbean islands, where green coloration is common. Substitute green (or olive) Fishair, Sili Legs, and chenille, and use olive grizzly hackle for the green version.

Mantis Shrimp Flies 65

Prey Species: Mantis Shrimp
Fly Pattern: Buz's Long Shrimp
Fly Type: Impressionistic

TIER: BUZ FENDER

Hook: Mustad Signature S71sss or Mustad 34007, sizes 2, 4
Body: Tan estaz (can also be tied in peach, chartreuse, white)
Wing: Tan craft fur (or color to match body)
Antennae: Black or peacock green Krystal Flash
Legs: Sili Legs, amber fleck or silver pearl, with red tips
Weight: $1/50$- or $1/100$-ounce dumbbell
Thread: Danville flat waxed nylon, color to match body
Weedguard: 20-pound-test Mason monofilament (can burn ends to make eyes)
Optional: Krystal Flash (color to match body) over the weedguard
Author Comments: This is a longer version (craft fur is considerably longer) of Buz's Shrimp, shown in chapter 8, Common Shrimp.

Prey Species: Mantis Shrimp
Fly Pattern: Bristle Worm
Fly Type: Impressionistic

TIER: CHRIS DEAN

Hook: Mustad 34007, size 2
Body: Tan Aunt Lydia's rug yarn, one wrap under wing to cock it up
Tail: Tan craft fur barred with an olive marker, orange Krystal Flash on top
Hackle: Natural brownish neck hackle clipped off on bottom
Eyes: Medium gold bead chain
Weedguard: 16-pound-test Mason monofilament, double beard
Thread: Flat waxed nylon, white
Tier Comments: This is a variation of Tim Borski's fly of the same name. It's a popular fly design for bonefish with variations from one tier to another. This is one of my variations. The fly looks very shrimplike in the water. Tied with the bead chain, it's a good fly for tailing or waking bonefish. For mudding fish in deeper water, I use a version with lead eyes ($1/50$, $1/36$ ounce).

Prey Species: Mantis Shrimp
Fly Pattern: Furry Mantis
Fly Type: Impressionistic

TIER: AARON ADAMS

Hook: Mustad 34007, size 2
Body: Light tan Slinky Fiber
Eyes: Burned 40-pound-test monofilament, ends blackened with a permanent marker
Wing: Two tan grizzly hackle, over which are six off-white round rubber legs barred with a permanent marker
Thread: Flat waxed nylon, pink

Tying Instructions
1. Tie in the hackle, claws, and eyes at the hook bend.
2. Pull a pencil-size strip of Slinky Fiber off the bundle, and cut it into approximately 2-inch sections.
3. Starting at the hook bend, tie in the sections of Slinky Fiber. First split the fiber bundles over the hook shank (so each side of the shank has an equal amount), and tie in with a figure-eight knot. Use one hand to smooth the fibers forward (toward the hook bend), while making a couple thread wraps at the tie-in location to keep the fibers leaning forward. Repeat this process, working your way toward the hook eye. Pack the bundles close together for a heavier body, farther apart for a lighter body.
4. After whip-finishing, comb and tease out the fibers and trim to shape.

CHAPTER 11

Snapping Shrimp
Alpheidae

Prey Type: Bottom-associated shrimp
Primary Habitats: Shallow coastal habitats, including seagrass beds, mangroves, sand and mud bottoms, oyster bars, and rubble
Geographic Range: Snapping shrimp occur in warm-temperate, subtropical, and tropical regions
Comments: Snapping shrimp have one enlarged claw with powerful muscles that can be used to make the claw snap shut with sudden force, hence, the snapping sound. The snapping sound is used in territorial defense and to stun prey, and an area with a lot of snapping shrimp will sound like an underwater popcorn machine. Snapping shrimp live in burrows in soft bottom or in crevices among oyster shells, rubble, or along beachrock shorelines, emerging from their hiding places to feed.

There are more than ten species of snapping shrimp in the regions covered in this book. All are similar is size and shape but tend to differ in color—coloration can even vary somewhat within a species based on habitat differences. Snapping shrimp are among the most common prey items for bonefish and to a slightly lesser extent for red drum. It is common for species of gobies to share the mantis shrimp's burrow, so where there are mantis shrimp, there are usually gobies.

Species: Banded Snapping Shrimp

Alpheus armillatus

Primary Habitats: Seagrass beds, rubble
Geographic Range: North Carolina to south Florida, Caribbean
Size Range: to 2 inches

Species: Common Snapping Shrimp

Alpheus heterochaelis

Primary Habitats: Oyster bars, rubble, seagrass
Geographic Range: North Carolina and Gulf of Mexico through Caribbean
Size Range: to 2 inches

Species: Red Snapping Shrimp

Alpheus armatus

Primary Habitats: Rubble, reefs
Geographic Range: South Florida, Caribbean
Size Range: to 2 inches

Species: Snapping Shrimp

Alpheus bouvieri

Primary Habitats: Seagrass beds, rubble, beachrock and rocky shorelines
Geographic Range: South Florida, Caribbean
Size Range: to 2 inches

Species: Snapping Shrimp

Alpheus estuariensis

Primary Habitats: Seagrass, rubble, oyster bars, mangroves
Geographic Range: Gulf of Mexico through Caribbean
Size Range: to 2 inches

Species: Snapping Shrimp

Alpheus paracrinitus

Primary Habitats: Seagrass, rubble
Geographic Range: South Florida, Caribbean
Size Range: to 2 inches

Species: Short-clawed Sponge Shrimp

Synalpheus brevicarpus
(two additional species are very similar in appearance)

Primary Habitats: All three species live in sponges
Geographic Range: North Carolina through Caribbean
Size Range: to 1 inch
Comments: On flats with sponges present, this may be a good prey to imitate. Its bright coloration may be one reason that the brightly colored ChiliPepper fly can be successful for bonefish.

Unidentified snapping shrimp, *Alpheus* sp.

FLIES

Prey Species: Snapping Shrimp
Fly Pattern: Craft Fur Clouser (tan or pink)
Fly Type: Impressionistic

TIER: AARON ADAMS

Hook: Mustad 34007, size 4 or 6
Wing: Tan or pink craft fur (aka fly fur), over pearl Krystal Flash, over white craft fur.
Weight: Small silver bead chain
Thread: Danville flat waxed nylon, pink
Tier Comments: This variation on the standard Clouser is great for bonefish. I think it easily mimics the light-colored snapping shrimp and other species of small shrimp that occur on the flats. I like to fish these in either tan/white or pink/white. Both do well on open sand bottom.

Prey Species: Snapping Shrimp
Fly Pattern: McVay Gotcha
Fly Type: Impressionistic

TIER: AARON ADAMS

Hook: Mustad 34007, size 4 or 6
Tail: Small pearl Mylar tubing, unfurled
Body: Pink thread under pearl body braid
Wing: Tan craft fur and pearl Krystal Flash
Weight: Silver bead chain
Thread: Danville flat waxed nylon, pink
Tier Comments: This standard pattern, originated by Jim McVay, should be in every bonefish angler's fly box. It works well for red drum and even striped bass when they are feeding on small shrimps. For bonefish, this pattern probably mimics snapping and mantis shrimp, and other species of small shrimp that occur on the flats. In more northern areas, this pattern likely imitates grass shrimp.

Snapping Shrimp Flies

Prey Species: Snapping Shrimp (as well as mantis and common shrimps)
Fly Pattern: Epoxy Mudbug
Fly Type: Impressionistic

TIER: ANDRIJ HORODYSKY

Hook: Gamakatsu SS15, size 2
Eyes: Large bead chain, black
Mouth: Small clump of natural/tan rabbit fur
Antennae: Two strands of tan Krystal Flash, tips colored red with a permanent marker
Legs: Four strands of tan Krystal Flash
Claws: Two pieces of natural/tan zonker strip
Underbody: Fourteen wraps of .025-inch lead wire, 20-pound-test monofilament frame, covered with clear 5-minute epoxy
Body: 5-minute epoxy mixed with three drops of tan Testor's ModelMaster acrylic paint
Swimmerets: One clump tan grizzly Chickabou
Thread: Danville 6/0, tan

Tying Instructions
1. With hook point up, tie in a pair of large black bead chain eyes under the hook shank opposite the hook point.
2. Tie in the rabbit mouth parts, Krystal Flash antennae and legs, zonker strip claws, and two pieces of monofilament to serve as the frame.
3. Add fourteen wraps of lead wire behind the bead chain eyes.
4. Pull the monofilament ends toward the hook eye and tie off, forming a teardrop shape that will serve as the frame for the epoxy. Whip-finish.
5. Coat the frame with clear 5-minute epoxy.
6. After the clear epoxy dries, mix 5-minute epoxy with tan Testor's ModelMaster acrylic paint, and coat the entire body. Place on a rotary wheel to dry.
7. After the epoxy dries, add the segmentation stripes with a brown permanent marker.
8. Tie in one small clump of grizzly Chickabou, with the tips just reaching the forward-most segmentation stripe, and whip-finish.

Tier Comments: Originally tied to mimic crayfish in freshwater, this pattern representes marine snapping shrimp, penaeid shrimp, and mantis shrimp that are important prey for coastal gamefishes. This pattern is lethal in mangrove, oyster reef, and surf habitats.

**Prey Species: Snapping Shrimp
(as well as mantis and common
shrimps)
Fly Pattern: Angora Shrimp
Fly Type: Impressionistic**

TIER: ANDRIJ HORODYSKY

Hook: Tiemco TMC811s, size 6
Eyes: Burned 20-pound-test monofilament, ends painted black with a permanent marker
Mouth: Small clump of ginger rabbit fur
Carapace: A thin strip of mottled bustard Thin Skin over a strip of tan 2-millimeter foam
Underbody: Eight wraps of .015-inch lead wire
Body: Dubbing loop of ginger Angora goat fur
Weight: Medium lead dumbbell
Thread: Danville 6/0, tan

Tying instructions
1. With hook point up, tie in the mouth parts and monofilament eyes.
2. Move the thread to the hook eye and tie in the lead eyes.
3. Tie in the strip of Thin Skin, followed by the foam strip.
4. Make eight wraps of lead wire around the hook shank.
5. Wrap the dubbing loop of Angora fur to the point on the shank directly opposite the hook point. Continue wrapping dubbing loop to hook eye; tie off.
6. Tightly pull the foam and Thin Skin carapace over the top of the Angora body. Tie off and trim.
7. Mix a small amount of clear 5-minute epoxy and apply to the Thin Skin.
8. Optional: Tie in the monofilament weedguard and whip-finish.

Tier Comments: This pattern represents marine snapping shrimp, common shrimp, and mantis shrimp that are important prey for coastal gamefish. This pattern is very effective in seagrass, mangrove, oyster bar, and surf habitats.

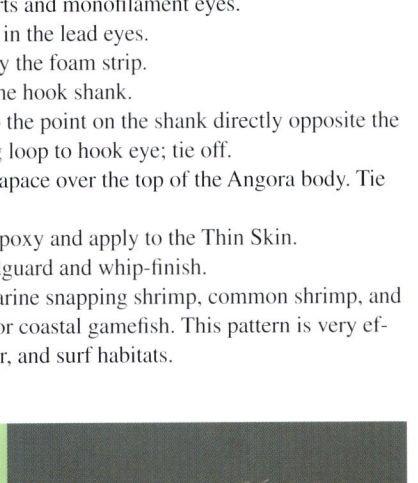

**Prey Species: Snapping Shrimp
Fly Pattern: Fernández Snapping Shrimp
Fly Type: Impressionistic**

TIER: AARON ADAMS

Hook: Mustad 34007, size 4 or 6
Wing: Brown craft fur
Butt: Orange yarn or chenille
Body: Tan yarn
Thread: Danville flat waxed nylon, brown

Tier Comments: I like to bend back the hook slightly, just behind the hook eye, so the wing is sure to make this fly weedless. This pattern, originated by Chico Fernández, is especially good on dark or grassy bottoms.

Snapping Shrimp Flies

Prey Species: Snapping Shrimp
Fly Pattern: Bonefish Special
Fly Type: Impressionistic

TIER: AARON ADAMS

Hook: Mustad 34007, size 4 or 6
Wing: White calf tail, outside of which are natural grizzly hackle tips (one each side)
Butt: Orange marabou
Underbody: Gold Mylar
Overbody: 20-pound-test monofilament
Thread: Danville flat waxed nylon, black

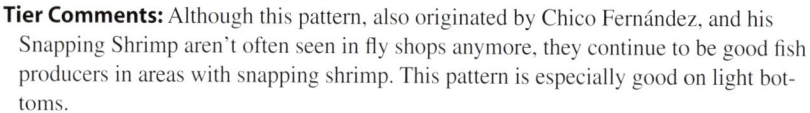

Tier Comments: Although this pattern, also originated by Chico Fernández, and his Snapping Shrimp aren't often seen in fly shops anymore, they continue to be good fish producers in areas with snapping shrimp. This pattern is especially good on light bottoms.

Prey Species: Snapping Shrimp
Fly Pattern: ChiliPepper
Fly Type: Impressionistic

TIER: AARON ADAMS

Hook: Mustad 34007, size 4
Wing: Orange craft fur, over blue Krystal Flash
Butt: Orange Krystal Flash
Underbody: Orange Mylar
Overbody: 20-pound-test monofilament
Thread: Danville flat waxed nylon, orange

Tier Comments: I'm not sure where I picked up this pattern many years ago, but it has worked for bonefish on occasion—especially on light-colored flats in the Caribbean. It took me a while to figure out why bonefish like it, but I thinkit is because it mimics the sponge shrimp (also bright orange) on flats that contain small sponges.

Prey Species: Snapping Shrimp
Fly Pattern: Furback Snapping Shrimp
Fly Type: Imitation

TIER: AARON ADAMS

Hook: Mustad 34007, size 2
Claw: Tip of a tan grizzly hackle
Forelegs: Tan marabou tips over pearl Krystal Flash
Eyes: Burned 30-pound-monofilament, ends blackened with Sharpie
Body: Medium tan chenille
Legs: Palmered tan grizzly hackle
Shellback: Shrimp-colored Kinky Fiber
Rostrum: Tips of Kinky Fiber used for shellback
Thread: Danville flat waxed nylon, white
Tying Tips: Start at the hook bend, where all materials are first tied in, and work your way toward the hook eye in sections to match the body segmentation. This is tied in the same fashion as the Krystal Shrimp (page 48).
Tier Comments: I call this the Furback Snapping Shrimp because I originally used craft fur for the shellback, but I like the look of the Kinky Fiber better.

Prey Species: Snapping Shrimp
Fly Pattern: Simple Snapping Shrimp
Fly Type: Impressionistic

TIER: AARON ADAMS

Hook: Mustad 34007, size 2
Claw: Tip of a tan grizzly hackle
Forelegs: Hackle barbs from the base of a tan grizzly hackle stem
Eyes: Burned 30-pound-monofilament, ends blackened with Sharpie
Body: Tan Aunt Lydia's sparkle yarn
Legs: Palmered tan grizzly hackle
Thread: Danville flat waxed nylon, white
Tier Comments: This is a simplified version of the Furback Snapping Shrimp and seems to work just as well.

CHAPTER 12

Grass Shrimp and Broken-back Shrimp
Palaemonidae and Hippolytidae

Prey Type: Bottom-associated shrimp
Primary Habitats: Shallow seagrass beds, oyster bars, and marshes
Geographic Range: Warm-temperate and subtropical regions from New England through the tropics
Comments: There are four species of grass shrimp in the regions covered in this book, two of which are shown here. Grass shrimp are so similar in appearance that it usually takes an expert to tell them apart. In subtropical and warm-temperate areas, they are present throughout the year. Based on the limited available data, however, they are most abundant during late winter and early spring. Coincidentally, this is when many other gamefish prey are in low abundance. This is also the time when they appear most often in gamefish stomachs. Any gamefish species that occurs in areas with grass shrimp will eat them, sometimes with abandon. I've caught speckled seatrout, for example, that are so full of grass shrimp that their stomachs are distended and they're regurgitating grass shrimp as they are brought to the boat. Despite having already overeaten, they were still hungry enough to take a grass shrimp fly. Striped bass and bluefish foraging in estuaries in spring also eat a lot of grass shrimp, and red drum to a lesser extent.

Broken-back shrimp are nearly identical in size and shape to grass shrimp but are not clear. The coloration of broken-back shrimp can vary somewhat with their habitat. Bonefish are probably the primary gamefish predators of broken-back shrimps.

These shrimp species are usually found clinging to and feeding among grass blades, marsh grass blades, or oyster shells. They generally aren't swimmers, like common shrimp (family Penaeidae) can be, but are often dislodged by currents and swept to gamefish waiting downstream.

GRASS SHRIMP

Species: Grass Shrimp
Palaemonetes pugio

Primary Habitats: Seagrass, drift algae, oyster bars
Geographic Range: New England to Florida, Gulf of Mexico
Size Range: to 1 1/2 inches
Comments: This is probably the most common grass shrimp in estuarine seagrass beds.

Species: Florida Grass Shrimp
Palaemon floridana

Primary Habitats: Seagrass, drift algae, oyster bars
Geographic Range: New England to Florida, Gulf of Mexico
Size Range: to 1 1/2 inches

BROKEN-BACK SHRIMP

Species: Eelgrass Broken-back Shrimp
Hippolyte zostericola

Primary Habitats: Seagrass
Geographic Range: South Florida, Caribbean
Size Range: to 1 inch
Comments: Broken-back shrimp are very similar in size to grass shrimp but tend to have coloration ranging from brown to bright green.

FLIES

Prey Species: Grass Shrimp
Fly Pattern: Palmered Hackle Shrimp
Fly Type: Impressionistic

TIER: AARON ADAMS

Hook: Mustad 34007, size 4
Tail: Olive grizzly hackle (2)
Body: Chartreuse thread under natural grizzly hackle, tied in at the hook bend and palmered to the hook eye
Weight: Small dumbbell eyes, tied in at the hook bend
Thread: Danville flat waxed nylon, chartreuse
Weedguard: 30-pound-test monofilament, ends burned to make eyes
Tier Comments: Grass shrimp don't have long pincers but do have antennae, so I use thin hackle for the tail to imitate the antennae.

Prey Species: Grass Shrimp
Fly Pattern: Spun Shrimp
Fly Type: Impressionistic

TIER: GLENN PITTARD

Hook: Mustad 34007, size 4
Eyes: $1/50$-ounce lead eyes
Body: Aunt Lydia's craft yarn, tan and orange
Tail: Orange Krystal Flash
Weedguard: 20-pound-test Mason monofilament

Tying Instructions
1. Tie in 10 to 12 strands of orange Krystal Flash.
2. Wrap thread forward and secure in the lead eyes.
3. Wrap thread back toward the hook point and create a dubbing loop. Insert teased out clumps of craft yarn. For a segmented look, I prefer to alternate the colors in the dubbing loop, a tuft of tan, then orange, tan, then orange, etc.
4. Wrap the dubbing loop forward, secure off at the eyes, and trim to shape. A small piece of Velcro glued to a popsicle stick makes the task of teasing the fibers easier.
5. Add a weedguard.

Tier Comments: This is a fairly simple pattern to tie. One of the things that I like about the fly is the ability to tease the spun fibers in order to create various styles of the same pattern.

Prey Species: Grass Shrimp
Fly Pattern: Cinnamon Shrimp
Fly Type: Impressionistic

TIER: GLENN PITTARD

Hook: Mustad 34007, size 2
Body: Medium pearl chenille, brown and tan hackle
Wing: Tan bucktail
Eyes: Monofilament
Thread: Brown nylon
Weedguard: 20-pound-test Mason monofilament
Tier Comments: I prefer this fly tied sparsely and fairly scruffy. This pattern can also be tied in olive.

Prey Species: Grass Shrimp
Fly Pattern: Gray Squirrel Bendback
Fly Type: Impressionistic

TIER: CHRIS HUMPHREY

Hook: Owner Mosquito, size 1/0
Tail: Copper Krystal Flash
Body: Barred tan chenille over lead wire wrapped on hook shank
Wing: Gray squirrel tail
Thread: Flat waxed nylon, gray

Tying Instructions
1. Tie in a small amount of Krystal Flash at the hook bend.
2. Tie in lead wire at the hook bend, and wrap three times down the hook shank.
3. Tie in chenille at the hook bend.
4. Secure the wire with thread wraps, wrap the chenille to the hook eye, and tie off.
5. Use pliers to slightly bend back the hook just behind the hook eye.
6. Tie in a matchstick-size clump of squirrel tail (fox tail is an alternative), use thread to build head, and whip-finish.

Tier Comments: This fly lands very quietly and can be used for tailing redfish and bonefish. The small amount of lead keeps the hook point up and the fly tracking straight. The weight also helps the fly perform well in areas with current. The fly can be fished in "washed out" potholes and scours around oyster bars, where current can affect the performance of other flies.

**Prey Species: Grass Shrimp
(and other small shrimps)
Fly Pattern: Mini Assassin
Fly Type: Impressionistic**

TIER: ANDRIJ HORODYSKY

Hook: Tiemco TMC 811s, sizes 6 and 8
Eyes: Medium bead chain, black
Mouth: Small clump of natural/tan rabbit fur
Antennae: Two strands of tan Krystal Flash, tips colored red with permanent marker
Legs: Four pieces of tan Zebra Legs
Head: Arizona hare's ear dubbing
Body: Tan turkey biot
Wing: Natural/tan rabbit fur
Thread: Danville 6/0, tan

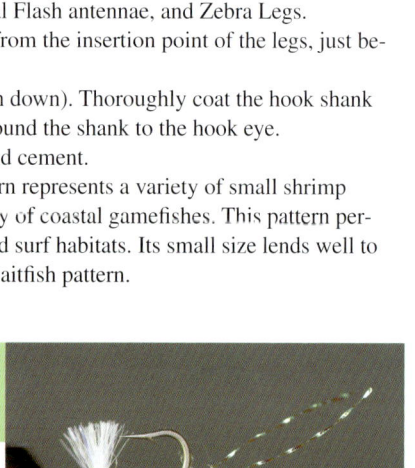

Tying Instructions
1. With the hook pointing upward, tie in a pair of medium black bead chain eyes under the shank opposite the hook point.
2. Tie in the rabbit fur mouth parts, Krystal Flash antennae, and Zebra Legs.
3. Dub the head of the fly with hare's ear from the insertion point of the legs, just behind the bead chain eyes.
4. Moisten the turkey biot and tie in (notch down). Thoroughly coat the hook shank with head cement, and wrap the biot around the shank to the hook eye.
5. Add the rabbit fur wing, whip-finish, and cement.

Tier Comments: This impressionistic pattern represents a variety of small shrimp species that are important prey for a variety of coastal gamefishes. This pattern performs very well in seagrass, mangrove, and surf habitats. Its small size lends well to being fished as a dropper behind a larger baitfish pattern.

**Prey Species: Grass Shrimp
Fly Pattern: Grass Shrimp
Fly Type: Impressionistic**

TIER: ANDRIJ HORODYSKY

Hook: Tiemco, TMC811s, sizes 6 and 8
Eyes: Medium bead chain, silver
Mouth: A small clump of white Z-lon
Antennae: Two strands of olive Mirror Accent Flash
Legs: Eight pieces of Super UV Flash
Underbody: Tan Danville thread, frame constructed from two pieces of 15-pound-test monofilament
Body: 5-minute epoxy mixed with three drops of silver Testor's ModelMaster acrylic paint
Thread: Danville 6/0, tan

SHRIMP

Tying Instructions
1. With the hook pointing upward, tie in a pair of medium bead chain eyes under the shank opposite the hook point.
2. Tie in the Z-lon mouth parts, Mirror Accent Flash antennae, and two pieces of monofilament to serve as the frame.
3. Directly opposite the hook point, tie in four pieces of Super UV Flash at their midpoint on the top of the hook shank. Create a post by pulling both ends upward and spiraling a base of thread around the base.
4. Pull the monofilament back toward the hook eye, tie off, and trim. This forms a small teardrop-shaped frame for the epoxy. Whip-finish.
5. Mix 5-minute epoxy with three drops of silver Testor's ModelMaster acrylic paint, and use this to coat the frame and thread wraps.

Tier Comments: This pattern represents grass shrimp and large opossum shrimp (*Mysis* sp) that are important prey for a variety of costal gamefish. This pattern performs very well in seagrass, mangrove, and surf habitats, and is especially deadly around pilings and dock lights at night. The small size of this pattern lends well to being fished as a dropper behind larger baitfish patterns.

Prey Species: Grass Shrimp
Fly Pattern: Grass Shrimp
Fly Type: Impressionistic

TIER: AARON ADAMS

Hook: Mustad 34007, size 6
Eyes: Small bead chain
Body: Medium pearl cactus chenille, palmered
Wing: White nylon hair (also acts as weedguard)
Thread: Flat waxed nylon, white

Prey Species: Grass Shrimp
Fly Pattern: Ultra Shrimp
Fly Type: Imitation

TIER: AARON ADAMS

Hook: Mustad 34007, size 4
Eyes: Burned 20-pound-test monofilament
Underbody: Tan or white thread
Forelegs: Tan Ultra Hair, tied in at the hook bend, pointing down
Legs: Palmered light brown grizzly hackle, trimmed on top
Body: Tan Ultra Hair, angled up, coated with 5-minute epoxy
Tail: Tag ends of the Ultra Hair used for the body
Thread: Flat waxed nylon, white
Tier Comments: This small version of the Ultra Shrimp, which was originated by Bob Popovics, remains the best grass shrimp imitation in my box.

Prey Species: Grass Shrimp
Fly Pattern: Dust Bunny
Fly Type: Impressionistic

TIER: AARON ADAMS

Hook: Mustad 34007, size 4
Eyes: Burned 20-pound-test monofilament, ends blackened with a Sharpie
Wing: Pearl Krystal Flash
Body: White sparkle yarn, wrapped around hook shank to taper from bend to eye, fibers teased out for legs
Thread: Flat waxed nylon, white

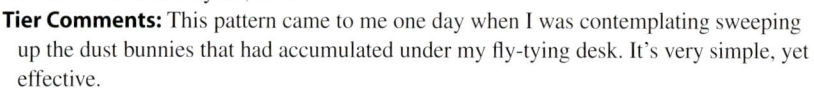

Tier Comments: This pattern came to me one day when I was contemplating sweeping up the dust bunnies that had accumulated under my fly-tying desk. It's very simple, yet effective.

Grass shrimp are very similar in appearance to small juvenile common shrimp. In fact, a couple grass shrimp species not shown here reach lengths large enough to be mistaken for small common shrimp. In addition, their behaviors are similar enough that many of the patterns (appropriately sized) are suitable for either group.

SECTION III
Bottom-associated *Prey Fish*

CHAPTER 13

Gobies
Gobiidae

Prey Type: Bottom-associated prey fish
Primary Habitats: Shallow coastal habitats, including seagrass beds, mangroves, sand and mud bottoms, and oyster bars
Geographic Range: Gobies are found in warm-temperate, subtropical, and tropical regions
Comments: Gobies are small, territorial, bottom-associated fish that are present in most shallow coastal habitats. For the species considered here, their coloration tends toward drab and generally matches their surroundings. Some species have burrows, while others protect crevices as territories. When out of their hiding places, they alternately dart about and rest on the bottom (their pectoral fins are modified to act as pedestals for them to rest on in a head-up orientation). When chased, they do not flee over long distances but move in short, darting motions, searching for a place to hide. Based on my field observations, I think that some of these species dive into soft sediment to escape predators. These characteristics are important when designing and fishing goby flies. The flies should be weighted (unless fishing in very shallow water), relatively thin-bodied, and earth-toned. Although most of the gobies listed here are small, I've found that it can be advantageous to tie goby flies that are a little bit longer than the naturals.

I've known snook, red drum, spotted seatrout, bonefish, and striped bass to eat gobies (from stomach contents), and all will take goby flies. As I mentioned in the introduction, gobies represent one of the prey groups that are untapped by fly anglers.

Species: Clown Goby

Microgobius gulosus

Primary Habitats: Shallow, soft-bottom estuarine habitats
Geographic Range: Mid-Atlantic to south Florida, Gulf of Mexico
Size Range: to 3 inches
Comments: This species is among the most common gobies in subtropical and warm-temperate middle-salinity estuarine habitats.

Photo on page 83: A mixture of seagrass and mangrove prop roots is a great place to find a wide variety of prey.

Species: Frillfin Goby

Bathygobius soporator

Primary Habitats: Shallow, often rocky, areas
Geographic Range: Florida and Bahamas, Gulf of Mexico, Caribbean
Size Range: to 3 inches
Comments: This is perhaps the most common species of goby in shallow, beachrock shoreline habitats in the tropics.

Species: Code Goby

Gobiosoma robustum

Primary Habitats: Shallow, protected seagrass and drift algae, in marine (high salinity) waters
Geographic Range: Florida, Gulf of Mexico
Size Range: to 2 inches

Species: Naked Goby

Gobiosoma bosci

Primary Habitats: Shallow, protected seagrass and algae-covered bottom, and oyster bars in estuaries
Geographic Range: New York to Florida, Gulf of Mexico
Size Range: to $2^1/_2$ inches
Comments: This species is common in shallow estuarine habitats of the warm-temperate region.

Species: Rockcut Goby

Gobiosoma grosvenori

Primary Habitats: Rubble, rocky shorelines, oyster bars
Geographic Range: North Carolina to Florida, Bahamas, Caribbean
Size Range: to 3 inches

Species: Dash Goby

Gobionellus saepepallens

Primary Habitats: Open sand, shares burrows with shrimp
Geographic Range: South Florida, Bahamas, Caribbean
Size Range: to 2 inches

© 2007 PAUL HUMANN / MARINELIFEIMAGES.COM

Species: Orangespotted Goby

Nes longus

Primary Habitats: Open sand
Geographic Range: South Florida, Bahamas, Caribbean
Size Range: to 4 inches

© 2007 NED DELOACH / MARINELIFEIMAGES.COM

Species: Bridled Goby

Coryphopterus glaucofraenum

Primary Habitats: Open sand, seagrass, rubble
Geographic Range: South Florida, Caribbean
Size Range: to 2 inches
Comments: This species is almost completely clear. When they are living over open sand bottom, there are usually no markings. Individuals living in seagrass beds often have brassy markings on the sides.

Species: Goldspot Goby

Gnatholepis thompsoni

Primary Habitats: Open sand, rubble, rocky bottom
Geographic Range: Florida, Bahamas, Caribbean
Size Range: to 3 inches
Comments: This species is one of the most abundant gobies in the tropical shallows.

FLIES

Prey Species: Gobies
Fly Pattern: Woolhead Goby
Fly Type: Impressionistic

TIER: AARON ADAMS

Hook: Mustad 34007, size 4
Body: Brown wool, spun
Wing: Brown hackle (tips cut out), over brown marabou, over copper Krystal Flash
Eyes: Small or medium brass barbell eyes
Thread: Danville flat waxed nylon, brown
Tier Comments: This fly is a general impressionistic pattern for gobies found on darker colored bottoms. I use this fly almost exclusively on open bottoms but will use a version with a weedguard in seagrass areas. The fly should be fished along the bottom in short, quick strips, interrupted by pauses.

Prey Species: Bridled Goby
Fly Pattern: Bridled Goby
Fly Type: Impressionistic

TIER: GINGER ALLEN

Hook: Mustad 34007, size 2
Tail: White fiber with pearl Awesome hair
Body: Dubbing loop of white and pearl Awesome hair
Head: Dubbing loop of white and silver Awesome hair
Eyes: Extra small white lead dumbbell
Thread: Gudebrod G, white
Tier Comments: This fly is designed to ride hook point up.

Prey Species: Dash Goby
Fly Pattern: Dash Goby
Fly Type: Impressionistic

TIER: GINGER ALLEN

Hook: Mustad 34007, size 2
Tail: Beige fiber with gold Awesome hair
Body: Beige fiber with gold Awesome hair mixed together in dubbing loop
Eyes: Small dumbbell yellow "real eyes"
Thread: Gudebrod 6/0, beige
Tier Comments: This fly is designed to ride hook point up.

Prey Species: Goldspot Goby
Fly Pattern: Goldspot Goby
Fly Type: Impressionistic

TIER: GINGER ALLEN

Hook: Mustad 34007, size 2
Tail: White fiber with pearl Awesome hair
Body: Dubbing loop of white and then brown fiber (two sections) mixed with gold Awesome hair
Eyes: Small dumbbell yellow "real eyes"
Thread: Gudebrod G, white
Tier Comments: This fly is designed to ride hook point up.

Prey Species: Orangespotted Goby
Fly Pattern: Orangespotted Goby
Fly Type: Impressionistic

TIER: GINGER ALLEN

Hook: Mustad 34007, size 2
Tail: Beige fiber with gold Awesome hair
Body: Orange and beige fiber mixed with gold Awesome hair in dubbing loop
Eyes: Extra small lead yellow dumbbell
Thread: Gudebrod 6/0, beige
Tier Comments: This fly is designed to ride hook point up.

Prey Species: Gobies
Fly Pattern: Craft Fur Clouser, chartreuse
Fly Type: Impressionistic

TIER: AARON ADAMS

Hook: Mustad 34007, size 4 or 6
Wing: Chartreuse craft fur (aka fly fur), over pearl Krystal Flash, over white craft fur
Weight: Small silver bead chain
Thread: Danville flat waxed nylon, chartreuse

Tier Comments: This variation on the Standard Clouser is great for bonefish feeding on open sand and seagrass bottoms. I think it probably mimics small, light-colored gobies that live in these habitats. The fly is best fished on the bottom, with short, halting strips. Use lead eyes for deeper water areas.

Prey Species: Gobies
Fly Pattern: Petrella's Brown Goby
Fly Type: Impressionistic

TIER: TONY PETRELLA

Hook: Eagle Claw 066SS 4XL, size 4
Eyes: Medium red bead chain
Body: Copper minnow-body tubing
Belly: Tan Hi-Viz
Flash: Gold Krystal Flash
Back: Bucktail dyed dark brown
Sides: Grizzly hackle dyed brown (two per side)
Face: Brown dubbing wrapped in a figure eight over and between the eyes
Thread: 3/0 monocord, brown

Prey Species: Gobies
Fly Pattern: Petrella's Champagne Goby
Fly Type: Impressionistic

TIER: TONY PETRELLA

Hook: Eagle Claw 066SS 4XL, size 4
Eyes: Medium red bead chain
Body: Copper minnow-body tubing
Belly: champagne polar fiber
Flash: Gold Krystal Flash
Back: Bucktail dyed dark brown
Sides: Grizzly hackle dyed brown (2 per side)
Face: Brown dubbing wrapped in a figure eight over and between the eyes
Thread: 3/0 monocord, brown

Prey Species: Gobies
Fly Pattern: Woolly Bugger Goby
Fly Type: Impressionistic

TIER: AARON ADAMS

Hook: Mustad 34007, size 2
Tail: Brown marabou, over which is root beer Krystal Flash
Underbody: Medium brown chenille
Overbody: Palmered brown hackle, clipped short
Weight: Medium gold barbell
Thread: Flat waxed nylon, brown

Goby Flies

CHAPTER 14

Blennies
Bleniidae

Prey Type: Bottom-associated prey fish
Primary Habitats: Shallow coastal habitats including seagrass beds, mangroves, sand and mud bottoms, and oyster bars
Geographic Range: Blennies occur in warm-temperate, subtropical, and tropical regions, although the blennies listed here are all from warm-temperate and subtropical regions
Comments: Blennies tend to be larger than gobies and live in similar habitats. Blennies also defend holes or crevices as territories. When not in their hiding places, they alternately rest on the bottom and move about in the area of their territory. Like gobies, coloration of most blennies in the areas listed above is earth-toned, but blennies have a higher body profile, so flies should be more bulky than goby imitations. Blennies are generally not as active as gobies. This behavior should be incorporated into fly design and presentation.

Blennies never occur in the top five diet items of gamefish according to scientific studies, probably because they are mostly preyed upon in shallow habitats not generally sampled in these studies. Based upon my observations, conversations with others, and diet lists from a few scientific studies, blennies do occur regularly in the diets of many gamefish, including snook, red drum, spotted seatrout, and bonefish.

Species: Florida Blenny

Chasmodes saburrae

Primary Habitats: Seagrass beds, mangroves, oyster bars
Geographic Range: Florida, eastern Gulf of Mexico
Size Range: to 4 inches
Comments: Within seagrass beds, Florida blennies prefer turtle grass over shoal grass.

Species: Striped Blenny

Chasmodes bosquianus

Primary Habitats: Oyster bars
Geographic Range: North Carolina to Florida, Northern Gulf of Mexico
Size Range: to 4 inches
Comments: Striped blennies tend to move to deeper water during winter, but during warmer months are common on shallow oyster bars. They are probably the most common shallow-water species of blenny in warm-temperate areas.

Species: Feather Blenny

Hypsoblennius hentzi

Primary Habitats: Oyster bars, rocky areas
Geographic Range: Mid-Atlantic to Florida, Gulf of Mexico
Size Range: to 4 inches

Species: Hairy Blenny

Labrisomus nuchipinnis

Primary Habitats: Shallow seagrass, rubble, beachrock shoreline
Geographic Range: Gulf of Mexico, Caribbean
Size Range: to 9 inches, usually smaller

Species: Unidentified Blenny

Labrisomus sp, whose size and coloration are similar for many species

Primary Habitats: Shallow seagrass, rubble, sandy and beachrock shorelines
Geographic Range: Caribbean
Size Range: to 4 inches

Blennies (Bleniidae)

Species: Crested Blenny

Hypleurochilus geminatus

Primary Habitats: Oyster bars
Geographic Range: North Carolina to Florida, Gulf of Mexico
Size Range: to 4 inches

FLIES

Prey Species: Crested Blenny
Fly Pattern: Crested Blenny Bunny
Fly Type: Imitation

TIER: GINGER ALLEN

Hook: Mustad 34007, size 1
Tail: 2-inch tan/brown barred rabbit strip, camouflage flash
Body: Dark brown satin "eyelash yarn"
Eyes: Gold-plated dumbbell
Thread: Gudebrod G, brown
Tier Comments: This fly is designed to ride hook point up.

Prey Species: Feather Blenny
Fly Pattern: Feather Blenny Bunny
Fly Type: Imitation

TIER: GINGER ALLEN

Hook: Mustad 34007, size 1
Tail: 2-inch olive/black barred rabbit strip
Body: Olive satin "eyelash yarn"
Eyes: Gold-plated dumbbell
Thread: Gudebrod G, black
Tier Comments: This fly is designed to ride hook point up.

Prey Species: Florida Blenny
Fly Pattern: Florida Blenny Bunny
Fly Type: Imitation

TIER: GINGER ALLEN

Hook: Mustad 34007, size 1
Tail: 2-inch light brown rabbit strip, camouflage flash
Body: Tan satin "eyelash yarn"
Eyes: Gold-plated dumbbell
Thread: Gudebrod G, brown
Tier Comments: This fly is designed to ride hook point up.

Prey Species: Blenny
Fly Pattern: Conehead Blenny
Fly Type: Impressionistic

TIER: AARON ADAMS

Hook: Mustad 34007, size 1, 2, or 4
Tail: Light brown fly fur (aka craft fur), gold Flashabou; add bars with permanent marker
Collar: Light brown marabou, palmered midshank
Head: Spun brown deer hair, cut to shape; brass cone (place the cone as the first step in tying this fly)
Tier Comments: The key to this fly is the way it is fished—it is designed to be bounced and scooted across the bottom. If a weedguard is desired, tie it in front of the brass cone as the final step.

Prey Species: Blennies
Fly Pattern: Petrella's Blenny
Fly Type: Impressionistic

TIER: TONY PETRELLA

Hook: Eagle Claw 066SS, size 4
Eyes: Gold dumbbell, size small or extra small
Flash: Gold Krystal Flash
Sides: Grizzly dyed brown (two feathers per side) plus one partridge feather per side
Thread: 3/0 monocord, brown

Blenny Flies

Prey Species: Blennies
Fly Pattern: Bendback Blenny
Fly Type: Impressionistic

TIER: AARON ADAMS

Hook: Mustad 34007, size 2 or 1; bend back shank near hook eye with pliers
Weight: Brass cone
Tail: Brown marabou, gold holographic Flashabou
Wing: Brown bucktail, outside of which are tan grizzly hackle (one on each side), over which is gold holographic Flashabou
Body: Medium brown chenille
Thread: Flat waxed nylon, brown

CHAPTER 15

Toadfishes
Batrachoididae

Prey Type: Bottom-associated prey fish
Primary Habitats: Seagrass, oyster bars
Geographic Range: Toadfishes occur in warm-temperate, subtropical, and tropical regions
Comments: Toadfish are rather sluggish and move only small distances at a time, so they are usually associated with some type of structure that will provide them shelter—oysters, seagrass, marsh grass, or mangrove prop roots. Flies that appear active as they are moved slowly along the bottom are good imitations of toadfish. This movement mimics the fin that runs along much of the dorsal surface and the fleshy tail. Thus, flies with marabou, rabbit, and other materials with inherent motion characteristics are common.

Although as adults toadfish grow rather large, juveniles are eaten by many gamefish. For example, toadfish are high on the menu of large bonefish in the Florida Keys and Bahamas. Juvenile toadfish are also eaten by red drum, snook, and spotted seatrout.

Species: Gulf Toadfish
Opsanus beta

Primary Habitats: Shallow seagrass beds, oyster bars
Geographic Range: South Florida, Gulf of Mexico
Size Range: to 12 inches
Comments: The top view (above right) is similar for all species shown here.

Species: Oyster Toadfish

Opsanus tau

Primary Habitats: Oyster bars, rocky bottom
Geographic Range: New England to Florida
Size Range: to 15 inches

Species: Belize Toadfish

Opsanus sp

Primary Habitats: Coral rubble, shallow seagrass
Geographic Range: Belize
Size Range: to 8 inches

FLIES

Prey Species: Toadfish
Fly Pattern: Woolly Toad
Fly Type: Imitation

TIER: AARON ADAMS

Hook: Mustad 34007, size 1 or 2
Tail: Tan craft fur, striped with brown Sharpie
Body: Tan wool, either spun or tied in clumps across the hook shank, trimmed to shape
Eye: Gold dumbbell eyes (sized to hook size) with black dot for pupil
Thread: Danville flat waxed nylon, tan or brown
Tier Comments: One option for the body is to alternate tan and brown wool to imitate the mottled/striped appearance of the toadfishes. Another option is to use tan wool and mark the body with a brown Sharpie.

Prey Species: Toadfish
Fly Pattern: Oyster Toadfish Conehead
Fly Type: Impressionistic

TIER: GINGER ALLEN

Hook: Mustad 34007, size 1/0
Tail: Brown deer hair, six ginger saddle, covered by two ginger grizzly or chinchilla saddle, camouflage flash
Body: Copper Mylar braid
Wing: Brown deer hair, camouflage flash, two ginger saddle, one grizzly saddle tied flatwing-style, six to eight peacock herl
Cheeks: Brown speckled hen coq de leon
Nose: Copper cone
Eyes: Gold 3D Mylar, epoxy in between
Thread: Gudebrod 6/0, beige
Weedguard: Bent leader wire

Prey Species: Toadfish
Fly Pattern: Gulf Toadfish Conehead
Fly Type: Impressionistic

TIER: GINGER ALLEN

Hook: Mustad 34007, size 1/0
Tail: Brown deer hair, six furnace saddle, covered by two furnace cock saddle, camouflage flash
Body: Copper Mylar braid
Wing: Brown deer hair, camouflage flash, three badger furnace saddle hackle tied flatwing-style, six to eight peacock herl
Cheeks: Black laced furnace hen hackle
Nose: Copper cone
Eyes: Gold 3D Mylar, epoxy in between
Thread: Gudebrod 6/0, beige
Weedguard: Bent leader wire

Prey Species: Toadfish
Fly Pattern: Marabou Toad
Fly Type: Impressionistic

TIER: AARON ADAMS

Hook: Mustad 34007, size 1
Tail: Brown and tan marabou, palmered simultaneously from the hook bend to halfway along the hook shank
Body: Spun wool, alternating between tan and brown
Weight: Gold barbell, eyes painted on
Thread: Danville flat waxed nylon, brown
Weedguard: If desired, 30-pound-test monofilament

Prey Species: Toadfish
Fly Pattern: Conehead Toad
Fly Type: Impressionistic

TIER: AARON ADAMS

Hook: Mustad 34007, size 2
Tail: Light brown fly fur (aka craft fur), barred with a black Sharpie
Body: Palmered light brown marabou, outside of which is gold holographic Flashabou
Head: One clump spun brown bucktail
Weight: Black conehead
Thread: Danville flat waxed nylon, brown
Weedguard: 30-pound-test monofilament
Tier Comments: I've done well with this fly in both seagrass and open bottom areas. The fly is good for sight-fishing if the fish aren't too spooky, or you can lead the fish by a few feet—wet marabou and the conehead weight make for a loud splashdown. This fly has also proven effective when blind-casting into open areas (potholes) in seagrass beds.

Prey Species: Gulf Toadfish
Fly Pattern: Toadfish
Fly Type: Impressionistic

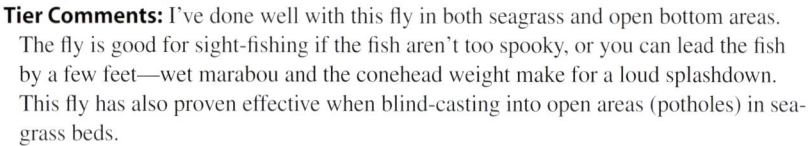

TIER: ANDRIJ HORODYSKY

Hook: Tiemco TMC 811s, size 4
Tail: Small clump of natural/variant rabbit fur, gold Wing N Flash, two split cree hackles
Body: Deer belly hair, spun, trimmed to shape; brown for back, white for abdomen
Wing: Small clump of natural/variant rabbit fur and monofilament weedguard (optional)
Weight/Eyes: Medium dumbbell, yellow with black pupil
Thread: Danville 6/0, tan
Tier Comments: This pattern represents the gulf toadfish and small gobies that constitute an underappreciated but surprisingly important part of the diet of large bonefish in the Florida Keys. In mid-Atlantic estuaries, this pattern also represents a variety of killifish, small drums, and gobies that are important prey for summer flounder, striped bass, bluefish, weakfish, red drum, and spotted seatrout.

CHAPTER 16

Grunts
Haemulidae

Prey Type: Bottom-associated prey fish
Primary Habitats: Shallow seagrass beds, mangrove shorelines
Geographic Range: Grunts occur in tropical and subtropical regions (primarily Caribbean, Florida), with the exception of the pigfish (see below).
Comments: Juveniles of many species of grunts are eaten by gamefish, but in my experience juveniles of the species listed below are the most common grunts eaten by gamefish and are found in shallow habitats frequented by fly anglers.

Juvenile grunts are most common in summer through fall and tend to hang together in loose schools near shelter (mangrove prop roots, seagrass) during the day. Most juvenile grunts have some yellow coloration. When chased, they tend not to move far. Juvenile grunts are eaten by jacks, snappers, groupers, bonefish, tarpon, and other gamefish.

Species: White Grunt

Haemulon plumieri

Primary Habitats: Seagrass beds, mangroves
Geographic Range: Cape Hatteras to Florida, Gulf of Mexico, Caribbean, but mostly subtropical and tropical areas
Size Range: Juveniles 1 to 6 inches

Species: Bluestriped Grunt

Haemulon sciurus

Primary Habitats: Seagrass beds, mangroves

Geographic Range: South Carolina to Florida, Caribbean, but mostly subtropical and tropical areas.

Size Range: Juveniles 1 to 6 inches

Species: Pigfish

Orthopristis chrysoptera

Primary Habitats: Seagrass beds, mud bottoms

Geographic Range: Mid-Atlantic to Florida, Gulf of Mexico

Size Range: to 6 inches

Comments: Pigfish is the one species of grunt that occurs exclusively in subtropical and warm-temperate areas. It is common in deeper seagrass beds from spring through fall and is smaller in spring, larger in fall. Pigfish are eaten by tarpon, red drum, and snook, and probably by other gamefish as well.

Species: French Grunt

Haemulon flavolineatum

Primary Habitats: Seagrass beds, mangroves
Geographic Range: South Carolina to Florida, Gulf of Mexico, Caribbean
Size Range: Juveniles 1 to 6 inches

FLIES

Prey Species: Pigfish
Fly Pattern: KB Pigfish Sr.
Fly Type: Imitation

TIER: KEN BAY

Hook: Mustad 9175, size 2/0
Wing: Puglisi fibers—ocean blue over white, marked with felt marker
Flash: Gold flecks
Eyes: Molded plastic
Thread: White nylon or fine mono

Tying Tips: The style in which I tie this fly is known as hi-tie; that is, all materials are tied on top of the hook. The white fibers are tied in at the hook bend, blue fibers forward, using 4-inch long sparse bunches. Irregular blotches are applied with a dark gray felt marker Prismacolor #PM115. With a light-bodied acrylic spray, apply a light coating on the fly and immediately sprinkle on glitter. Then spray a second coat of acrylic. Be generous with the glitter because much will shed. Repeat process on the other side of the fly. For more durability, immediately after applying the glitter, lay the fly flat, and with a firm piece of plastic treated with a coating of nondrying spray like Pam, press the entire fly to firmly set the glitter.

Tier Comments: I was encouraged that I had come up with a good likeness of the pigfish by an experience I had at an outdoor show where I was tying flies. My booth was next to a bait and tackle shop that was the only supplier of pigfish on a regular basis in this area. When I showed him my KB Pigfish, he liked them so much he cleaned me out of all that I had. I accepted this as an endorsement of my fly.

Prey Species: Pigfish
Fly Pattern: KB Pigfish Jr.
Fly Type: Imitation

TIER: KEN BAY

Hook: Mustad 9175, size 1/0
Wing: Puglisi fibers—ocean blue over white, marked with dark gray felt marker (#PM115 Prismacolor)
Back: Gold and olive Puglisi fibers
Flash: Gold flecks
Eyes: $1/4$-inch molded plastic
Thread: White nylon

Tier Comments: All fibers are tied on the hook hi-tie style, white fibers at the hook bend, blue fibers forward, using 3-inch long sparse bunches. Gold glitter is applied after combing and trimming fly to shape. Glitter applied as described for Pigfish Sr. (see above).

Grunt Flies

Prey Species: Grunts
Fly Pattern: Clouser Minnow
Fly Type: Impressionistic

TIER: AARON ADAMS

Hook: Mustad 34007, size 1 or 2
Body: Blue bucktail, over yellow bucktail, over pearl Krystal Flash, over white bucktail
Thread: Danville flat waxed nylon, yellow
Weight: Medium dumbbell eyes, silver

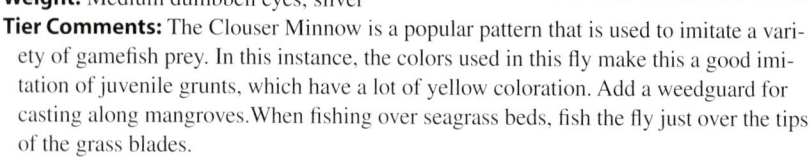

Tier Comments: The Clouser Minnow is a popular pattern that is used to imitate a variety of gamefish prey. In this instance, the colors used in this fly make this a good imitation of juvenile grunts, which have a lot of yellow coloration. Add a weedguard for casting along mangroves. When fishing over seagrass beds, fish the fly just over the tips of the grass blades.

Prey Species: Grunts
Fly Pattern: Lefty's Deceiver
Fly Type: Imitation

TIER: AARON ADAMS

Hook: Mustad 34007, size 1
Tail: Two yellow saddle hackles outside two white saddle hackles, curved inward
Wing: Blue, over yellow, over white bucktail; pearl flashabou
Thread: Danville flat waxed nylon, chartreuse

Tier Comments: The Deceiver is a popular pattern that is used to imitate a variety of gamefish prey. In this instance, the colors used in this fly make this a good imitation of juvenile grunts, which have a lot of yellow coloration. Fish as described above for the Clouser Minnow. Since barracuda are common catches with this pattern, a wire bite tippet is suggested.

CHAPTER 17

Snappers
Lutjanidae

Prey Type: Bottom-associated prey fish
Primary Habitats: Juveniles of many snapper species occupy shallow habitats such as seagrass beds, mangrove shorelines, oyster bars, and rubble.
Geographic Range: Although some shallow-water snapper species can be found in warm-temperate waters, especially in summer, the species listed here (and most likely to be eaten by gamefish) are tropical and subtropical.
Comments: As adults, many species of snappers can be great fun on fly, but juvenile snappers fall prey to larger fish. Although there are more than a dozen species of snapper in our area, there are only a few species whose juveniles are found in shallow waters and that I have observed in gamefish stomachs.
  Jacks, barracuda, tarpon, bonefish, and snook are probably the major gamefish predators of juvenile snappers.

Species: Yellowtail Snapper

Ocyurus chrysurus

Primary Habitats: Seagrass beds and mangroves (for juveniles)
Geographic Range: Most common Florida and Caribbean, also present to Cape Hatteras and Gulf of Mexico
Size Range: Juveniles most commonly eaten at 1 to 6 inches
Comments: Juvenile yellowtail snapper is the only snapper I have seen in gamefish stomachs on multiple occasions (other species only once or twice). Jacks, barracudas, and other snappers are probably the main gamefish predators of juvenile yellowtail snapper, but bonefish and tarpon also eat them.

Species: Mangrove (aka Gray) Snapper

Lutjanus griseus

Primary Habitats: Seagrass beds and mangroves (for juveniles)
Geographic Range: Most common in Florida and Caribbean, also present to Cape Hatteras and Gulf of Mexico
Size Range: Juveniles most commonly eaten at 1 to 6 inches
Comments: Juvenile mangrove snapper can be very abundant along mangrove shorelines (and to a lesser extent in seagrass beds) in south Florida and the Caribbean.

FLIES

Prey Species: Yellowtail snapper
Fly Pattern: Lefty's Deceiver
Fly Type: Imitation

TIER: AARON ADAMS

Hook: Mustad 34007, sizes 1 to 2/0
Tail: Six white hackles, with a few strands of pearl Krystal Flash
Overwing: Yellow bucktail
Underwing: White bucktail (with a sparse bunch of yellow bucktail along the midline), with a few strands of pearl and yellow Krystal Flash
Eyes: Stick-on prism
Thread: Danville flat waxed nylon, white
Tier Comments: This is obviously a particular color pattern of the famous Lefty's Deceiver, a pattern well recognized for its effectiveness. This version is most effective over seagrass areas more than 4 feet deep, with the fly fished in the lower half of the water column.

CHAPTER 18

Drums
Sciaenidae

Prey Type: Bottom-associated prey fish
Primary Habitats: Shallow coastal habitats, including seagrass beds, mangroves, sand and mud bottoms, and oyster bars
Geographic Range: Drums occur in warm-temperate, subtropical, and tropical regions
Comments: These species all feed on small animals living in or on the bottom, so they are most common over soft-bottom habitats. The juvenile sizes are most often eaten by gamefish, though some larger gamefish do feed on adults. In subtropical and warm-temperate areas, juvenile spot and croaker are most abundant in spring, whereas juvenile kingfish are most common in summer. All of these species are eaten by red drum. Along southeastern U.S. beaches, for example, kingfish (aka whiting) are high on the red drum's menu. In Florida, snook also prey on whiting. Striped bass and bluefish also feed on spot, croaker, and whiting. In the tropics, snook and barracuda feed on small sciaenids along sandy beaches.

Species: Spot

Leiostomus xanthurus

Primary Habitats: Bays and estuaries, usually over sparsely vegetated or open bottom, oyster bars, marsh creeks (especially as juveniles)
Geographic Range: New England to northeast Florida, Gulf of Mexico
Size Range: to 14 inches

Species: Kingfish (aka whiting), three nearly identical species

Menticirrhus spp

Primary Habitats: Beaches
Geographic Range: Throughout warm-temperate, subtropical, and tropical regions
Size Range: to 18 inches

Species: Croaker

Micropogonias undulatus

Primary Habitats: Bays and estuaries, usually over sparsely vegetated or open bottom, oyster bars, marsh creeks (especially as juveniles)
Geographic Range: New England to Florida, Gulf of Mexico
Size Range: to 20 inches

FLIES

Prey Species: Whiting
Fly Pattern: Whiting Half-and-Half
Fly Type: Imitation

TIER: AARON ADAMS

Hook: Mustad 34007, size 1/0
Tail: Six white hackles, curved inward
Body: White bucktail on bottom, pearl Flashabou in middle, grey bucktail on top
Weight: Large silver dumbbells
Thread: Danville flat waxed nylon, white
Tier Comments: This is a half-and-half with colors appropriate to a whiting. The best retrieve is to skip or skid the fly along the bottom. I like this fly for large snook along the beach in summer in south Florida (a color variation is good for striped bass along beaches in New England and the mid-Atlantic).

Prey Species: Whiting
Fly Pattern: Woolhead Whiting
Fly Type: Imitation

TIER: AARON ADAMS

Hook: Mustad 34007, size 1/0
Tail: White marabou plume, pearl Flashabou
Body: Spun white wool, trimmed to shape
Weight: Large silver dumbbells
Thread: Danville flat waxed nylon, white
Tier Comments: The marabou, wool, and lead eyes combine to make this a less than stealthy fly to cast. However, it gets to the bottom quickly, so it is good for fishing along beaches that are a little too steep to use lighter weight flies.

CHAPTER 19

Porgies
Sparidae

Prey Type: Bottom-associated prey fish
Primary Habitats: Shallow seagrass beds and oyster bars
Geographic Range: New England to Florida, Gulf of Mexico, Caribbean
Comments: This family includes numerous species of round-bodied fish that are relatively common in coastal and nearshore habitats. However, only the habitats of interest to fly anglers are listed here. The following two species listed are nearly identical in appearance, with pinfish inhabiting warm-temperate and subtropical regions, and sea bream in the tropics.

Species: Pinfish

Lagodon rhomboides

Primary Habitats: Shallow seagrass beds and oyster bars
Geographic Range: New England to Florida, Gulf of Mexico. Most common south of Cape Hatteras, North Carolina, and north of the Florida Keys
Size Range: to 14 inches (typical size eaten by gamefish: 3 to 6 inches)
Comments: Juvenile pinfish first occur in estuaries in late winter and early spring, and although numerous, seem to be too small to be worth the effort of gamefish—these small juvenile pinfish are not abundant in gamefish diets. From midspring through fall, however, they are numerous and in the right size range, so they are eaten by many gamefish. Red drum, snook, spotted seatrout, and tarpon all readily eat pinfish. Numerous gamefish focus on this prey during the fall migration of subadult pinfish from estuaries.

Species: Sea Bream

Archosargus rhomboidalis

Primary Habitats: Shallow seagrass beds, mangrove shorelines
Geographic Range: Mid-Atlantic and northeastern Gulf of Mexico through Caribbean, but mostly Caribbean
Size Range: to 13 inches (typical size eaten by gamefish: 3 to 6 inches)
Comments: Sea bream are nearly identical in appearance to pinfish (above), and their main geographic range is from the Florida Keys southward. Sea bream live in seagrass beds and along mangrove shorelines, but I've found the juveniles to be most common in areas where seagrass grows up to the mangrove edge. Any pattern to imitate pinfish will also be a good imitation of sea bream.

FLIES

Prey Species: Pinfish
Fly Pattern: KB Pinfish
Fly Type: Imitation

TIER: KEN BAY

Hook: Mustad 9175, size 1/0
Wing: Sky blue Puglisi fibers, blue and yellow Krystal Flash
Belly: White Puglisi fibers
Eyes: 1/4-inch red/black stick-on
Thread: White nylon or fine monofilament

Tying Instructions

1. On the body, make the vertical stripes with a gray felt marker (#PM115 Prismacolor), and use a black Sharpie for opercular spot.
2. The yellow Krystal Flash is made by staining pearl Krystal Flash with a yellow felt marker (#PM19 Prismacolor).
3. Use sparse 3-inch bunches of Puglisi fibers.
4. On each side use three strands each of blue and yellow Krystal Flash, tied in just behind the head.

5. Use your forefinger to spread a thin layer of Flex-Loc over the Krystal Flash on the body (optional).
6. The Puglisi fibers must be combed during construction and trimmed to pinfish shape.
7. This fly can also be tied naturally weedless by using a jig-style hook (see bottom photo on previous page).

Tier Comments: Jim Grace, a Florida Gulf coast guide, liked this fly when he spotted it on my table at a show, and his recommendations have resulted in orders from as far away as Wyoming by people heading to Florida to fish.

Author Comments: Pinfish are also abundant in the northern Gulf of Mexico, and this pattern can also be used to imitate small sea bream in the tropics.

Prey Species: Pinfish
Fly Pattern: Oscar's Pinfish
Fly Type: Imitation

TIER: OSCAR FELIU

Hook: Mustad C71S SS, size 3/0
Tail: Six to eight white saddle hackles about 4 inches long, mixed with pearl Flashabou
Skirt: White calf hair to flank the saddle hackles
Underbody: Sparse Artic fox tail hair mixed with Wing N Flash (repeat this step to build the body)
Veil: Puglisi sea fibers over pearl Wing N Flash
Top: Olive-green sea fibers, over pearl/green Wing N Flash
Eyes: $3/8$-inch 3D eyes, affixed to transparent plastic and tied on with thread
Thread: 3/0 monocord or Danville A+, white
Finish: Olive stripes and the touch of gold near the belly made with permanent markers; cover the head and the eyes with fast-drying epoxy

Tier Comments: The size and coloration of this prey fish changes from summer to winter. I don't know of an inshore gamefish that doesn't feed on pinfish at some point during the year. If you are hunting for jacks, spotted seatrout, or redfish, a fly 2 to 3 inches long will do, but for snook or tarpon, you may want to increase the size to 5 or 6 inches.

Prey Species: Pinfish
Fly Pattern: Bendback Pinfish
Fly Type: Imitation

TIER: AARON ADAMS

Hook: Mustad 34007, size 1/0 or 2/0; hook bent backward just behind hook eye
Underwing: White Kinky Fiber
Overwing: Alternated yellow and sky blue Kinky Fiber
Eyes: 3/8-inch yellow prismatic stick-on
Thread: Flat waxed nylon, white
Flash: Pearl Wing N Flash, applied outside the wing
Head coating: A layer of Softex applied from the thread wraps to just behind the hook eye
Tier Comments: This fly is tied hi-tie style, with all material on the hook point side of the forward portion of the hook shank (i.e., in front of the new bend). This makes the fly weedless, which is essential because pinfish and sea bream are usually associated with seagrass. Care must be taken not to spread the Softex back too far—this will cover the hook point.

SECTION IV

Midwater Prey Fish

CHAPTER 20

Wrasses and Parrotfishes
Labridae and Scaridae

Prey Type: Midwater prey fish
Primary Habitats: Shallow coastal habitats including seagrass beds, mangroves, sand and mud bottoms
Geographic Range: Wrasses occur in warm-temperate, subtropical, and tropical regions, but in my experience are more common as gamefish prey in the tropics and subtropics.
Comments: This is another of the untapped groups of gamefish prey. Since they mostly use their pectoral fins rather than their caudal (tail) fin for swimming, wrasses swim with a jerky motion similar to how some species of birds fly—with each move forward, they also move up and down. When chased, however, they dart away quickly, and often dive into cover such as seagrass.

Jacks, snappers, and groupers are probably the main gamefish predators of wrasses and parrotfish, but other gamefish, including bonefish, also eat them.

WRASSES

Species: Slippery Dick

Halichoeres bivittatus

Primary Habitats: Backreef flats, rubble and mixed seagrass–rubble bottom around reefs
Geographic Range: North Carolina to Florida, Gulf of Mexico, Caribbean, but mostly in tropical regions
Size Range: to 8 inches
Comments: Only the "supermales," shown here, take on brighter coloration. Otherwise, slippery dicks are a bland tan with a long black stripe down each side. They are very common in rubble–seagrass areas and backreefs.

Photo on page 111: A seagrass flat on an early rising tide is perfect for using flies that imitate resident bottom-associated prey.

Species: Pearly Razorfish

Hemipteronotus novacula

Primary Habitats: Open sand bottom
Geographic Range: North Carolina to Florida, Gulf of Mexico, Caribbean, but mostly in tropical regions
Size Range: to 9 inches

© 2007 PAUL HUMANN / MARINELIFEIMAGES.COM

Species: Rosy Razorfish

Hemipteronotus martinicensis

Primary Habitats: Open sand bottom
Geographic Range: South Florida, Bahamas, Caribbean
Size Range: to 6 inches
Comments: Razorfishes are most common in sandy areas (sometimes mixed with other habitats) because they bury in the bottom to avoid predators—they hover a few inches off the bottom and dive into the sand when approached.

© 2007 PAUL HUMANN / MARINELIFEIMAGES.COM

This unknown wrasse is a good example of the general coloration of numerous species of wrasses with camouflage coloration that inhabit shallow seagrass beds in the tropics.

PARROTFISH

Species: Bucktooth Parrotfish

Sparisoma radians

Primary Habitats: Seagrass beds
Geographic Range: South Florida, Caribbean
Size Range: to 8 inches, generally smaller
Comments: These parrotfish are common in shallow seagrass beds. When pursued, they first try to outswim the predator, darting back and forth just above the grass blades, and then dive into the cover of the seagrass at the last minute to escape.

Wrasses and Parrotfishes (Labridae and Scaridae)

FLIES

Prey Species: Slippery Dick
Fly Pattern: Clouser Minnow
Fly Type: Imitation

TIER: AARON ADAMS

Hook: Mustad 34007, sizes 2 to 1/0
Wing: Tan bucktail over black Krystal Flash, over white bucktail
Eyes: Dumbbell eyes, ends painted black
Thread: Danville flat waxed nylon, tan
Tier Comments: This fly is obviously the well-known standard fly designed by Bob Clouser. The fly is best fished near the bottom over rubble and seagrass (a mix of these habitats is best), generally in water more than 3 feet deep. Retrieve the fly to give it an erratic forward and up-and-down motion. This is a good fly for jacks around patch reefs and along deeper backreefs.

Prey Species: Pearly Razorfish
Fly Pattern: Pearly Razorfish
Fly Type: Imitation

TIER: GINGER ALLEN

Hook: Mustad C71S, size 1/0
Tail: White fiber mixed with pearl Awesome hair
Body: Two sections of white fiber mixed with pearl Awesome hair; then same mixture dubbed to hook eye, topped with clear, hard plastic cut-out, coated with epoxy mixed with pearl artist Pulver dust
Eyes: Silver 3D Mylar or pearl vinyl paint
Thread: Clear monocord
Weedguard: 20-pound-test Hard Mason monofilament
Author Comments: This and the following two razorfish patterns are dead-on imitations and promise to become go-to flies for fishing deeper sand and sand-with-sparse-seagrass bottoms near reefs in the tropics.

Prey Species: Rosy Razorfish
Fly Pattern: Female Rosy Razorfish
Fly Type: Imitation

TIER: GINGER ALLEN

Hook: Mustad C71S, size 1/0
Tail: White fiber mixed with pearl Awesome hair
Body: One section of rust fiber mixed with yellow Awesome hair, one section of white fiber mixed with pearl Awesome hair; then white/pearl mixture dubbed to hook eye, topped with clear, hard plastic cut-out, coated with epoxy mixed with pearl artist Pulver dust
Eyes: Gold 3D Mylar or gold vinyl paint
Thread: Clear monocord
Weedguard: 20-pound-test Hard Mason monofilament

Prey Species: Rosy Razorfish
Fly Pattern: Male Rosy Razorfish
Fly Type: Imitation

TIER: GINGER ALLEN

Hook: Mustad C71S, size 1/0
Tail: White fiber mixed with pearl Awesome hair
Body: Two sections of white fiber mixed with pearl Awesome hair; then same mixture dubbed to hook eye, topped with clear, hard plastic cut-out, coated with yellow vinyl paint; then epoxy
Eyes: Gold 3D Mylar or gold vinyl paint
Thread: Clear monocord
Weedguard: 20-pound-test Hard Mason monofilament

CHAPTER 21

Mojarras
Gerreidae

Prey Type: Midwater prey fish
Primary Habitats: Shallow coastal habitats, including seagrass beds, mangroves, sand and mud bottoms, and oyster bars
Geographic Range: Warm-temperate, subtropical, and tropical regions
Comments: Since they mostly eat detritus (decaying organic matter) and small organisms in the sediments, mojarras are mostly associated with soft-bottom areas. They alternately hover over the bottom, move short distances quickly, and tip their heads down to take mouthfuls of sediment. When chased, they swim rapidly across the bottom. I think some species may burrow in the bottom when chased. Although they don't form schools, mojarras tend to be abundant in areas where they occur (you'll never come across just one).

Since mojarras are bottom-oriented species, it can be advantageous to use weighted flies or intermediate line when fishing unweighted mojarra imitations. Alternatively, when sight-fishing in shallow water with mojarra imitations, I use an unweighted fly (for a softer landing) and try to cast the fly far enough in front of the fish that the fly has enough time to sink to the bottom before I begin the retrieve.

I've split the mojarras into two groups based on body shape. The first group, low body profile, are all very similar in shape, size, and coloration. In fact, it is difficult to differentiate many of the species, all of which are in the same genus (*Eucinostomus*). This group of species is present in most shallow coastal habitats, and are often one of the most abundant species. Because of their silver coloration and body shape, they can be imitated rather well with many herring imitation flies (chapter 26).

The second group has a higher body profile. Although these species are similar in shape, they differ in color. The key with these patterns is to have flies with high body profiles.

Although they rarely show up in scientific diet studies, I think that most coastal gamefish eat mojarras when given the chance. I've observed mojarras eaten by bonefish, red drum, snook, spotted seatrout, tarpon, barracuda, and bluefish, in habitats ranging from beach to sand flat to mangrove creek. This is probably because mojarras are among the most common fish species in these soft-bottom habitats.

LOW BODY PROFILE MOJARRAS

Species: Silver Jenny
Eucinostomus gula

Primary Habitats: Shallow seagrass beds, mangrove and marsh shorelines, and mangrove and marsh creeks
Geographic Range: New England to Florida, Gulf of Mexico, Caribbean
Size Range: to 7 inches, usually smaller

Species: Slender Mojarra
Eucinostomus jonesi

Primary Habitats: Beaches, sand flats, high salinity seagrass beds
Geographic Range: Florida, Caribbean
Size Range: to 8 inches, usually smaller

Species: Spotfin Mojarra
Eucinostomus argenteus

Primary Habitats: Shallow seagrass beds, mangrove lagoons, marshes, oyster bars, beaches, sand flats
Geographic Range: Mid-Atlantic to Florida, Gulf of Mexico, Caribbean
Size Range: to 8 inches, usually smaller

Species: Mottled Mojarra
Eucinostomus lefroyi

Primary Habitats: Beaches, sand flats
Geographic Range: North Carolina to Florida, Gulf of Mexico, Caribbean
Size Range: to 9 inches, usually smaller

Mojarras (Gerreidae)

Species: Tidewater Mojarra

Eucinostomus harengulus

Primary Habitats: Brackish water shallow seagrass beds, mangrove creeks, marshes
Geographic Range: Florida, Gulf of Mexico
Size Range: to 7 inches, usually smaller

Species: Bigeye Mojarra

Eucinostomus havana

Primary Habitats: Shallow coastal marine habitats
Geographic Range: Florida, Caribbean
Size Range: to 7 inches, usually smaller

HIGH BODY PROFILE MOJARRAS

Species: Yellowfin Mojarra

Gerres cinereus

Primary Habitats: Open sand bottom, seagrass beds, near coral reefs, beaches, mangrove lagoons
Geographic Range: South Florida, Gulf of Mexico, Caribbean
Size Range: to 16 inches, usually smaller

Species: Striped Mojarra

Diapterus plumieri

Primary Habitats: Brackish water mangroves, marshes, bays
Geographic Range: South Carolina to Florida, Gulf of Mexico, continental Caribbean (not on most islands)
Size Range: to 12 inches, usually smaller
Comments: The Irish pompano (*Diapterus auratus*) is nearly identical to the striped mojarra but is entirely silver (it lacks the striping that shows up faintly in the photo).

MIDWATER PREY FISH

LOW BODY PROFILE MOJARRA FLIES

Prey Species: Silver Jenny
Fly Pattern: Silver Jenny Streamer
Fly Type: Imitation

TIER: GINGER ALLEN

Hook: Mustad C71S, size 1/0
Tail: White marabou, pearl flash
Body: Gudebrod pearl Mylar HT braid
Wing: White deer hair, pearl flash, six white saddle hackle
Head: Pearl metallic thread
Eyes: Pearl/black vinyl paint, or silver Mylar
Thread: Gudebrod G, white

Prey Species: Any low body mojarra
Fly Pattern: Conehead Mojarra
Fly Type: Imitation

TIER: AARON ADAMS

Hook: Mustad 34007, size 1 or 2
Body: White Kinky Fiber
Eyes: Stick-on eyes, style of your choice
Weight: Silver cone
Thread: Flat waxed nylon, white
Tier Comments: This is a bendback pattern to make the fly weedless and to hide the hook. Prior to sliding on the cone, use pliers to bend the hook shank just behind the hook eye. Tie all the Kinky Fiber on the portion of the hook shank between the new bend and the hook eye.

Other fly patterns

Other patterns that are shown in other sections of this book are also good imitations of low body profile mojarras. These include Skok's Mushmouth Variant and Doug Hedges White Beach Fly (under herrings in section V).

HIGH BODY PROFILE MOJARRA FLIES

Prey Species: Any High-bodied Mojarra (striped mojarra, yellowfin mojarra)
Fly Pattern: Mojarra Hi-Tie
Fly Type: Imitation

TIER: AARON ADAMS

Hook: Mustad 34007, size 2/0
Body: Wing N Flash or similar, pearl; color with permanent marker if desired
Eyes: Stick-on eyes, style of your choice
Thread: Flat waxed nylon, white

Tying Instructions
1. Bend back the hook at a point about halfway between the hook eye and bend. This makes the body form around the hook point. The material is alternated between the straight section of the hook shank behind the hook eye.
2. Tie in small bunches of the Wing N Flash hi-tie style, starting at the bend you made in the hook and working forward to the hook eye. Bunches should be tied on both the top and underside of the hook shank. The hi-tie style gives the fly a high vertical profile. Use small bunches and don't use too much material. The trick is to use enough material to make the impression of a striped mojarra, but not so much material to make the fly bulky.
3. Whip-finish the head, and trim the body to shape.
4. Apply stick-on eyes, and cover the head region with Softex from the hook eye to just behind the stick-on eyes. This helps to keep the eyes on the fly even after numerous fish are caught and helps to keep the high profile shape of the fly.
5. Use permanent markers to add colors as appropriate for each species.

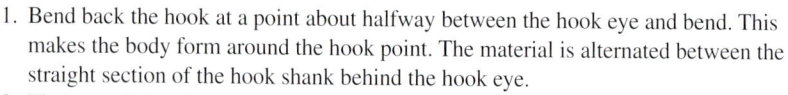

Tier Comments: I tie this fly bendback style to make it naturally semiweedless, a must when fishing mangrove shorelines and seagrass beds. The materials are tied hi-tie style on both sides of the hook shank to give the fly a high profile and make the fly weedless.

Prey Species: Mojarra
Fly Pattern: Oscar's Beach Dweller
Fly Type: Imitation

TIER: OSCAR FELIU

Hook: Mustad Signature C47S D, sizes 6 and 4
Underbody: Pearlescent Flashabou, two strands per side
Body: Puglisi sea fibers, very sparse, white for the belly and light brown or beige for the top
Eyes: 3D, affixed to the sea fibers with super glue
Thread: Danville A+, white
Finish: Coat head and eyes with epoxy
Tier Comments: The beach dwellers seem to inhabit the shallow trough in the surf zone along sandy beaches. They are on the bottom of the trough, where they seem to be constantly feeding, and have see-through beige or sandy coloration. From what I have observed, these are a prey of preference for snook.
Author's Comments: Based on Oscar's description and his fly pattern, he was seeing mojarras.

CHAPTER 22

Killifishes, Mollies, and Mosquitofish
Cyprinodontidae and Poeciliidae

Prey Type: Midwater prey fish (also use bottom- and upper-water habitats)
Primary Habitats: Shallow coastal habitats, including seagrass beds, mangroves, salt marsh, sand and mud bottoms, and oyster bars
Geographic Range: Killifishes occur in warm-temperate, subtropical, and tropical regions; mollies and mosquitofish are mostly found in subtropical and tropical regions.
Comments: If you fish in marsh or mangrove habitats, you must have flies to imitate killifish. Killifishes are among the most common small fishes in shallow, soft-bottom protected habitats throughout the area. They are especially prominent in warm-temperate and subtropical regions. Muddy shorelines, mangroves, salt marshes, and protected oyster bars all host at least one species of killifish. Although not schooling species per se, they do tend to occur in groups.

In warm-temperate and subtropical marshes and mangroves, they tend to be dull earthy colors. In the tropics and areas with clearer water, they tend to be lighter shades. The one exception to this is that killifishes in very muddy water with very low visibility (e.g., South Carolina marsh creeks) are often very pale. The males of many species take on brighter coloration during breeding season (usually spring) and can get careless about predators in their attempts to woo females.

Any gamefish that occurs in areas with killifishes will eat them. In fact, in salt marsh and mangrove creeks of warm-temperate and subtropical areas, killifishes are usually the number one prey fish found in gamefish stomachs. This includes snook, red drum, spotted seatrout, tarpon, striped bass, and bluefish.

KILLIFISHES

Species: Sheepshead Minnow
Cyprinodon variegatus

Primary Habitats: Shallow seagrass beds, mangrove and marsh shorelines, and mangrove and marsh creeks
Geographic Range: New England to Florida, Gulf of Mexico, Caribbean
Size Range: to 3 inches
Comments: These photos show how coloration changes based on habitat differences. The fish in the top photo was captured in a tannin-stained, dark-bottom creek, and the fish in the bottom photo was captured in clear water over a light bottom. These color differences also occur in other killifish species.

Species: Rainwater Killifish
Lucania parva

Primary Habitats: Seagrass beds, mangroves, marsh
Geographic Range: New England to Florida, Gulf of Mexico
Size Range: to $1\frac{1}{2}$ inches

Species: Diamond Killifish
Adinia xenica

Primary Habitats: Shallow seagrass beds, mangroves, marshes
Geographic Range: Gulf of Mexico
Size Range: to $1\frac{1}{2}$ inches

Killifishes, Mollies, and Mosquitofish (Cyprinodontidae and Poeciliidae)

Species: Goldspotted Killifish

Floridichthys carpio

Primary Habitats: Mangroves, marshes, oyster bars
Geographic Range: South Florida, Gulf of Mexico
Size Range: to 2½ inches

Species: Gulf Killifish

Fundulus grandis

Primary Habitats: Brackish water shallow seagrass beds, mangrove creeks, marshes
Geographic Range: Florida, Gulf of Mexico
Size Range: to 7 inches

Species: Mummichug

Fundulus heteroclitus

Primary Habitats: Brackish water shallow seagrass beds, marshes
Geographic Range: New England to northeast Florida
Size Range: to 5 inches
Comments: Identical in appearance to gulf killifish, mummichug have a different geographic range.

Species: Striped Killifish

Fundulus majalis

Primary Habitats: Shallow seagrass beds, muddy bays, marshes
Geographic Range: New England to northeast Florida, Gulf of Mexico
Size Range: to 7 inches

Species: Marsh Killifish

Fundulus confluentus

Primary Habitats: Brackish water mangrove and marsh creeks, bays, and grassbeds
Geographic Range: Mid-Atlantic to Florida, Gulf of Mexico
Size Range: to 3 inches

Species: Longnose Killifish

Fundulus similis

Primary Habitats: Mangroves, shallow open-bottom bays
Geographic Range: South Florida
Size Range: to $4^{1}/_{2}$ inches

Killifishes, Mollies, and Mosquitofish (Cyprinodontidae and Poeciliidae)

Species: Saltmarsh Topminnow

Fundulus jenkinsi

Primary Habitats: Marshes
Geographic Range: Gulf of Mexico
Size Range: to 2 1/2 inches

Species: Bayou Killifish

Fundulus pulvereus

Primary Habitats: Brackish water shallow bays, marshes
Geographic Range: Gulf of Mexico
Size Range: to 3 inches

Species: Spotfin Killifish

Fundulus luciae

Primary Habitats: Marshes
Geographic Range: New England to North Carolina
Size Range: to 1 1/2 inches

MOLLIES AND MOSQUITOFISH

Species: Sailfin Molly

Poecilia latipinna

Primary Habitats: Shallow mangrove and marsh creeks
Geographic Range: Cape Hatteras to Florida, Gulf of Mexico, Caribbean
Size Range: to 5 inches

Species: Mosquitofish

Gambusia holbrooki

Primary Habitats: Brackish to fresh water, shallow mangrove and marsh creeks
Geographic Range: Mid-Atlantic to Florida, Gulf of Mexico
Size Range: to 1 1/2 inches

FLIES

Prey Species: Killifishes (also mollies and mosquitofish)
Fly Pattern: Mangrove Muddler, brown and olive versions
Fly Type: Impressionistic

TIER: AARON ADAMS

Hook: Mustad 34011, size 4
Tail: Brown (or olive) bucktail under gold holographic Flashabou (or olive Angel Hair)
Body: Gold body braid wrapped around the hook shank, under 15-pound-test monofilament wrapped around the hook shank
Head: Brown (or olive) bucktail spun, trimmed to shape
Thread: Danville flat waxed nylon, brown (or olive)
Weedguard: 20-pound-test Ande monofilament
Tier Comments: This fly is a simplified adaptation of the classic Muddler. Since some of the killifishes live oriented toward the bottom and others live close to the water surface, it is a good strategy to have unweighted and weighted versions. For the weighted version, slide a gold conehead onto the shank before starting to tie the fly. For the brown version, all of the deer hair used in this pattern is from the back side of a bucktail (the part of the bucktail that is rarely used). It's important to use a loop knot to attach this fly to the tippet—this allows the fly to wobble between strips.

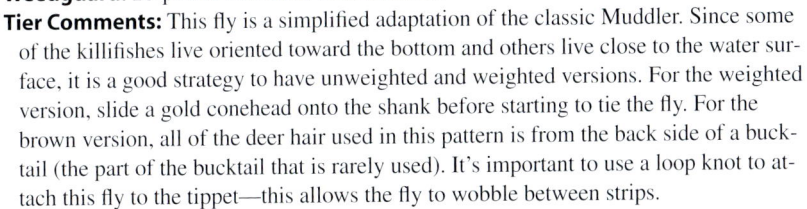

Prey Species: Mummichug
Fly Pattern: Woolly Mummi
Fly Type: Imitation

TIER: AARON ADAMS

Hook: Mustad 34007, size 1
Tail: Olive and tan craft fur (barred with Sharpie markers) over gold holographic Flashabou
Body: Olive and tan wool, spun
Eyes: $3/16$-inch Hologram Dome eyes, gold
Thread: Danville flat waxed nylon, olive
Weedguard: 20-pound-test Ande monofilament
Tier Comments: Mummichugs are not very flashy; in fact, they are rather drab in color, so there is little flash in this pattern (the flash is an underlayer). Mummichugs are common in swampy areas (salt marsh and mangrove) and are identical in coloration to gulf killifish.

Killifish, Molly, and Mosquitofish Flies

Prey Species: Killifishes
Fly Pattern: Mangrove Minnow
Fly Type: Imitation

TIER: DOUG HEDGES

Hook: Mustad 34007, size 4
Wing: Tan craft fur mixed with gold flash
Head: Tan craft fur coated with Softex
Eyes: 3D prism eyes
Thread: Danville flat waxed nylon, brown
Weedguard: 17-pound-test Hard Mason doubled monofilament
Tier Comments: Color these as needed to match local prey, using permanent marker to color the back.

Prey Species: Longnose Killifish
Fly Pattern: Longnose Killifish
Fly Type: Impressionistic

TIER: GINGER ALLEN

Hook: Mustad C71S, size 1/0
Tail: Black marabou with holographic silver flash
Body: Holographic silver braid
Wing: White bucktail above and below; 4 black saddle hackle covered by 2 grizzly saddle hackle
Eyes: Silver holographic
Head: Silver metallic thread coated with epoxy
Thread: Gudebrod G, black
Tier Comments: Longnose also resembles bayou killifish.

Prey Species: Killifish
Fly Pattern: Bendback
Fly Type: Impressionistic

TIER: GLENN PITTARD

Hook: Mustad 34007, size 1 or 2
Eyes: Painted or stick-on
Body: Flashabou wrapped with monofilament
Wing: Fishair, choice of colors as shown
Thread: Color to match fly

Tying Instructions

1. Start by applying a slight bend to the hook just behind the hook eye.
2. Cut a length of monofilament (16-pound-test works well).
3. Tie in the monofilament and leave a gap behind the hook eye. Hold the monofilament against the shank, and cover it with thread wraps all the way to the hook bend.
4. Move the thread back up to the hook eye, and tie in four to six strands of Flashabou.
5. Wrap the Flashabou down the hook shank and then back up and tie off.
6. At this stage I like to add a little mottling to the Flashabou by dotting it here and there with a permanent black marker.
7. Make tight wraps of the mono up the hook shank toward the eye and tie off.
8. There are a variety of color choices to use as a wing, depending on the species being imitated.
9. Using small clumps of fiber, build a wing.
10. Build a head with thread, whip-finish, and coat with epoxy if desired.
11. Paint on eyes after a coat of epoxy, and then cover with fingernail polish. (Stick-on prism eyes could be used rather than paint.)

Prey Species: Killifish
Fly Pattern: Kinky Mangrove Minnow
Fly Type: Impressionistic

TIER: AARON ADAMS

Hook: Mustad 34007, size 1
Eyes: Stick-on prismatic
Wing: Tan over white Kinky Fiber; use a permanent marker to draw vertical bars
Thread: Danville flat waxed nylon, white
Tier Comments: The colors of this fly can be changed to match local killifish species. This color combination has worked well in locations where the killifish are light colored, such as longnose killifish and sheepshead minnows.

Prey Species: Killifish
Fly Pattern: Olive Seaducer
Fly Type: Impressionistic

TIER: AARON ADAMS

Hook: Mustad 34007, size 1
Wing: Small bunch of olive bucktail to prevent hackle from fouling; gold holographic Flashabou; two pair olive grizzly hackle, curved outward
Collar: Palmered olive grizzly hackle
Thread: Danville flat waxed nylon, olive
Tier Comments: This longstanding standard pattern has been used to imitate a variety of gamefish prey. In this instance, the size and color closely match many species of killifish.

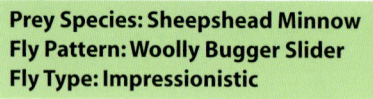

Prey Species: Sheepshead Minnow
Fly Pattern: Woolly Bugger Slider
Fly Type: Impressionistic

TIER: AARON ADAMS

Hook: Mustad 34007, size 1
Wing: White marabou, bars made with a black Sharpie
Underbody: 1/8-inch-thick fly foam, white
Overbody: Pearl crystal chenille
Hackle: Palmered natural grizzly hackle
Thread: Danville flat waxed nylon, white
Tier Comments: When in the water, the vertical barring of sheepshead minnows is an obvious characteristic. They tend to stay near the surface and leap out of the water when being chased by gamefish. This fly is a variation on the standard Woolly Bugger that swims just under the surface and has the general coloration and size to mimic a sheepshead minnow.

Prey Species: Killifish
Fly Pattern: Grizzly Bendback
Fly Type: Impressionistic

TIER: AARON ADAMS

Hook: Mustad 34007, size 1 (hook shank bent just behind the hook eye)
Eyes: Stick-on prismatic
Underwing: Olive over white bucktail; root beer Krystal Flash
Overwing: One tan grizzly hackle on each side
Thread: Danville flat waxed nylon, white

Prey Species: Killifish
Fly Pattern: Olive Clouser Minnow
Fly Type: Impressionistic

TIER: AARON ADAMS

Hook: Mustad 34007, size 1
Weight: Brass dumbbells, medium
Underwing: White bucktail
Overwing: Olive bucktail over root beer Krystal Flash
Thread: Danville flat waxed nylon, olive
Tier Comments: This standard is perhaps one of the most used patterns in saltwater fly fishing. This color combination can be used in many situations, but I tend to use it when fishing in areas with killifish. It is popular in the northeastern United States but is underutilized in the estuarine waters of the southeast and Gulf of Mexico.

Prey Species: Killifish
Fly Pattern: Olive and White Bendback
Fly Type: Impressionistic

TIER: CHRIS DEAN

Hook: Mustad 34007, size 2/0; use needle-nose pliers to bend the hook into a bendback-style
Body: Gold Mylar overwrapped with clear Rexlace or Swannundaze
Wing: Peacock herl over olive bucktail over white bucktail; gold Flashabou on the sides; wing should be 3 inches long
Head: Brown thread
Eyes: Painted on, black over yellow
Thread: Flat waxed nylon, brown
Tier Comments: This is a variation of the fly pattern Prince of Tides. It is designed to imitate the dark-colored prey fish in the backcountry areas of the Everglades. Weedless flies are important for the areas that I fish, where a weedless fly can be pulled over a submerged log or through underwater vegetation.

Killifish, Molly, and Mosquitofish Flies

CHAPTER 23

Eels
Anguillidae

Prey Type: Midwater prey fish
Primary Habitats: Eels have a complex life cycle that spans from open ocean to freshwater rivers. The juvenile life stage is best suited to imitation with a fly. Juveniles live in nearshore coastal and estuarine habitats and are most common in summer through fall.
Geographic Range: Warm-temperate and subtropical regions

Species: American Eel

Anguilla rostrata

Primary Habitats: Juveniles live in nearshore coastal and estuarine habitats; adult live in freshwater but migrate to the ocean to spawn.
Geographic Range: Warm-temperate and subtropical waters of North and South America
Size Range: to 3 feet, but typical juvenile sizes for imitation with a fly are 3 to 6 inches.
Comments: Juveniles are most common in estuarine habitats during summer. They swim with a snakelike sinuous motion.

FLIES

Prey Species: American Eel
Fly Pattern: Zonker Eel
Fly Type: Impressionistic

TIER: AARON ADAMS

Hook: Owner 5170-121, size 2/0
Tail: Olive zonker strip
Collar: Palmered olive zonker strip
Thread: Danville flat waxed nylon, olive
Tier Comments: Thanks to Capt. Les Hill for keying me in on subadult tarpon's appetite for juvenile American eels. This is especially the case in estuaries during summer.

132   **MIDWATER PREY FISH**

Prey Species: American Eel
Fly Pattern: Oscar's Mini-bait
Fly Type: Imitation

TIER: OSCAR FELIU

Hook: Mustad S71 SS, sizes 6, 4, and 2
Tail: A few strips of pearlescent Mylar
Keel: A triangular piece of lead sheet
Belly: White Enrico's sea fibers (or similar) mixed with pearlescent micro fibers; just enough to cover the keel and long enough to go beyond the hook's bend
Top: Olive fibers, same length as the belly
Eyes: 3D eyes affixed to clear plastic, tied in with thread
Weedguard: 20-pound-test Hard Mason monofilament
Thread: Danville A+, white
Finish: Coat of fast-drying epoxy on the head and eyes
Tier Comments: This is a generic pattern for imitating small eels. This fly rides hook point up. Barbell eyes can be substituted for a keel for weight.

Prey Species: Eel
Fly Pattern: FisHead Sandeel
Fly Type: Impressionistic

TIER: JACK GARTSIDE

Hook: Daiichi 2546, Mustad 34007 or similar, sizes 2 to 6
Tailwing: Thin olive (or other appropriate color) saddle feathers
Flash: Pearl or olive GSS or Mylar
Skirt: Olive marabou
Fishhead: $1/4$-inch or $1/3$-inch white or chartreuse Corsair tubing colored on top and along lateral line with water-resistant olive marker
Thread: Danville 6/0, white or olive
Author Comments: Jack submitted this fly as a sandeel imitation, but I've included the fly here because I think with a couple of modifications (color, change to a tarpon-size hook), it will make a good juvenile American eel imitation.

Eel Flies

SECTION V
Baitfish

CHAPTER 24

Anchovies
Engraulidae

Prey Type: Baitfish
Primary Habitats: Anchovies occur in the upper portions of the water column in numerous open estuarine and coastal habitats, most often in open areas (e.g., bays) rather than constrained areas (e.g., creeks).
Geographic Range: Tropical, subtropical, and warm-temperate waters
Comments: Combined with silversides, anchovies are often referred to as glass minnows. By and large, flies that imitate anchovies are also good imitations of silversides, so they are interchangeable. In fact, many of the flies shown here could have been listed under silversides just as easily. One difference is that, in general, anchovies have more of a tannish hue and silversides an olive hue on their dorsal (top) surface.

Anchovies are schooling species that are seasonally abundant in warm-temperate areas, reaching peak abundance in fall. In the subtropics their peak abundance extends through winter. They are common throughout the year in the tropics, with peak abundances probably occurring in spring and fall (based on my experience). Although more than a dozen species occur in our area, only the species most likely to be encountered by fly anglers are listed here. The species listed here are all very similar in appearance, with differences mostly determined by micro-characteristics such as fin location and number of fin rays. The bay anchovy, however, has a higher body profile than the slimmer Cuban and striped anchovies, which can be accounted for in fly design. I think it's the slimmer species that are most often fed upon by coastal speedsters such as little tunny and Atlantic bonito.

Most gamefish will eat anchovies given a chance, even gamefish considered bottom feeders, such as bonefish and red drum. In addition, large schools of anchovies that are present in summer and fall attract larger predators, such as tarpon, who eat them by the mouthful.

Species: Striped Anchovy

Anchoa hepsetus

Primary Habitats: Although occurring in multiple open water habitats, beach is the primary habitat. Striped anchovies are found entirely in marine areas, not in estuaries.

Photo on page 135: Birds can help you locate gamefish feeding on baitfish.

Geographic Range: Chesapeake Bay to central Florida, Gulf of Mexico, South America (probably not along tropical islands)
Size Range: to 6 inches, but usually smaller, at least in shallow coastal waters
Comments: The anchovy on the bottom of the photograph, a juvenile that only recently metamorphosed from a larval form, lacks a side stripe and is clear except for its abdomen.

Species: Bay Anchovy

Anchoa mitchilli

Primary Habitats: Most open water coastal habitats, usually in relatively shallow areas
Geographic Range: New England to Florida, Gulf of Mexico
Size Range: to 4 inches
Comments: This is the species most often found in estuaries. Bay anchovies have a higher body profile than the other anchovy species listed here.

Species: Cuban Anchovy

Anchoa cubana

Primary Habitats: Multiple open water habitats; beach is the primary habitat. They tend to remain in shallow waters, except along the Gulf Coast where they apparently migrate inshore-offshore.
Geographic Range: Gulf of Mexico, northeast Florida, to Caribbean
Size Range: to 3 inches

Species: Dusky Anchovy

Anchoa lyolepis

Primary Habitats: Multiple open water habitats; beach is the primary habitat. Dusky anchovies occur in shallow bays and inlets but do not venture into low salinity areas (they may migrate in and out of inlets with the tide to avoid low salinity water).
Geographic Range: Gulf of Mexico and southeast Florida to Venezuela
Size Range: to 3½ inches

Anchovies (Engraulidae)

FLIES

Prey Species: Anchovy
  (also silversides, small herrings)
Fly Pattern: Anchovy
Fly Type: Impressionistic

TIER: GLENN PITTARD

Hook: Mustad 34007, size 2
Body: Pearl body braid
Wing: Pearl Flashabou, peacock herl
Thread: White nylon
Tier Comments: This is a good pattern when gamefish are focused on small anchovies (and small silversides). Add a weedguard of 20-pound-test monofilament for fishing along mangrove shorelines.

Prey Species: Bay or Striped Anchovy
Fly Pattern: Popovics's Jiggy
Fly Type: Impressionistic

TIER: DAVE SKOK

Hook: TMC 777SP, size 4
Cone: Small silver Jiggy head or cone (make two turns of .030-inch lead wire on the shank and slide into the head)
Wing: White bucktail, over which are 2 or 4 strands of Herring Blue UV Krystal Flash, over which is a sparse amount of pink bucktail
Author Comments: This pattern and this color combination have proven deadly for me when fishing for false albacore.

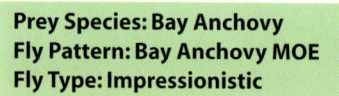

Prey Species: Bay Anchovy
Fly Pattern: Bay Anchovy MOE
Fly Type: Impressionistic

TIER: GINGER ALLEN

Hook: Mustad 34007, size 2
Body: Extra small silver bead chain dumbell, white thread built up in diamond shape, epoxy mixed with silver holographic ultra fine glitter
Wing: White Super Hair, silver flash
Head: Silver metallic thread
Thread: Gudebrod G, white
Tier Comments: Originators of this fly are A. J. Hand and Lefty Kreh.

BAITFISH

Prey Species: Anchovy
Fly Pattern: Bucktail Blonde
Fly Type: Impressionistic

TIER: AARON ADAMS

Hook: Mustad 34007, size 2
Body: Pearl diamond braid, tied in at the hook bend, palmered forward to the hook eye
Tail: White bucktail
Wing: Olive bucktail, over root beer Krystal Flash, over yellow bucktail
Thread: Danville flat waxed nylon, white
Tier Comments: This is a Joe Brooks pattern that has stood the test of time. It is a popular sandeel pattern in the Northeast but does well as an anchovy imitation in more southern waters. It can be tied in a variety of color combinations and sizes to imitate numerous baitfish, including silversides and herrings.

Prey Species: Anchovy
Fly Pattern: Oscar's Beach Darter
Fly Type: Imitation

TIER: OSCAR FELIU

Hook: Mustad C71S SS, sizes 8, 6, and 4
Tail: A few Wing N Flash fibers 1 inch in length, pearl and blue
Underbody: Two fibers per side of pearlescent Flashabou
Body: Puglisi fibers tied sparsely; white for the belly and blue for the top; trimmed to a long taper
Eyes: 3D eyes, super glued to the sea fibers
Thread: Danville A+, white
Finish: Coat the head and eyes with fast-drying epoxy (optional)
Tier Comments: When on the beach, one can see very small fish (anchovies) swimming in the surface waters of the trough created by the waves as they roll unto the beach. These fish seem to be forever in motion, moving in and out with the waves. They are elongated in shape and have a blue iridescence to them. They were the inspiration for this pattern.

Prey Species: Anchovy (also silverside)
Fly Pattern: Glass Minnow
Fly Type: Imitation

TIER: CHRIS DEAN

Hook: Mustad 34007, size 4
Body: Silver Mylar overwrapped with clear 40-pound-test monofilament
Belly: White craft fur, $1^{1}/_{2}$ inches long
Wing: Four strands of black Krystal Flash, over light green Krystal Flash, over tan craft fur $1^{1}/_{2}$ inches long
Eyes: Painted on, black over yellow

Anchovy Flies

Head: White thread coated with clear nail polish
Thread: Flat waxed nylon, white
Tier Comments: I created this variation of a Chico Fernández pattern in the late 1980s. I wanted the silver body to be the centerline of the fly instead of the belly. The glass minnows that we use for chum and are abundant locally have a silver stripe down their sides.

Prey Species: Anchovy
Fly Pattern: Kinky Fiber Anchovy
Fly Type: Imitation

TIER: AARON ADAMS

Hook: Mustad 34007, size 2
Wing: Tan over white Kinky Fiber, tied in behind the hook eye
Stripe: Silver Flashabou
Eyes: Hologram eyes, $3/16$ inch
Overcoat: Silicone, two coats (apply the side stripe between coats)
Thread: Flat waxed nylon, white

Prey Species: Anchovy
Fly Pattern: Epoxy Forage
Fly Type: Imitation

TIER: ADRIJ HORODYSKY

Hook: Tiemco TMC 811s, sizes 6 and 8
Eyes: $1/8$-inch yellow prismatic
Abdomen: 5-minute epoxy mixed with three drops silver Testor's ModelMaster acrylic paint
Underwing: Super UV Flash under white craft fur
Overwing: Tan craft fur
Coating: Clear 5-minute epoxy over body and hook shank
Thread: Danville flat floss, pink
Tier Comments: Color variations of this pattern can be tailored to represent a variety of small baitfish species. The anchovy version is lethal in all estuarine and coastal conditions. Impressionistic chartreuse, pink, and tutti-fruiti combinations are also effective. An all-black or all-purple version works well at night.

CHAPTER 25

Silversides
Atherinidae

Prey Type: Baitfish
Primary Habitats: The upper portions of the water column in most coastal habitats
Geographic Range: Tropical, subtropical, and warm-temperate waters
Comments: Along with anchovies, silversides are commonly referred to as glass minnows. All silversides are very similar in appearance. Silversides are schooling species and can be found in most shallow habitats encountered by fly anglers. They tend to be most abundant in warm-temperate waters from spring through fall and are abundant in subtropical and tropical regions throughout the year. To varying degrees, they serve as prey for most coastal gamefish. Silversides are usually the "glass minnow" species found in estuarine creeks and can also be common along tropical shorelines.

Species: Tidewater Silverside

Menidia peninsulae

Primary Habitats: Seagrass, mangroves, salt marsh, and beaches
Geographic Range: Florida, much of the Gulf of Mexico
Size Range: to 6 inches
Comments: Tidewater silversides are probably the most common silverside in backcountry habitats throughout their range and are present throughout the year.

Species: Hardhead Silverside

Atherinomorus stipes

Primary Habitats: Beaches
Geographic Range: Caribbean, including south Florida and the Bahamas
Size Range: to 4 inches
Comments: Hardhead silversides are common in open, marine, coastal waters of the tropics. This is the species of silverside that anglers are most likely to encounter along tropical beaches.

Silversides (Atherinidae)

Species: Inland Silverside

Menidia beryllina

Primary Habitats: Tidal and freshwater mangroves and salt marsh
Geographic Range: Massachusetts to Florida, Gulf of Mexico
Size Range: to 4 inches
Comments: Almost identical in appearance to tidewater silversides, inland silversides are really only present in areas that are always low in salinity, streams where they have access to upstream low salinity areas throughout the year, or areas where tidewater silversides are absent.

Species: Atlantic Silverside

Menidia menidia

Primary Habitats: Salt marsh and beaches
Geographic Range: New England to northeast Florida
Size Range: to 6 inches
Comments: Atlantic silversides are most abundant in marine waters along beaches and near inlets in warm-temperate areas.

FLIES

Prey Species: Silversides (also anchovies)
Fly Pattern: Bendback
Fly Type: Impressionistic

TIER: AARON ADAMS

Hook: Mustad 34007, size 1, bendback hook (i.e., away from hook point) about $1/4$ inch behind hook eye
Body: Pearl braid, wrapped from hook bend to $1/4$ inch behind hook eye
Wing: White bucktail
Flash: Pearl Krystal Flash (plus a couple strands of copper for tannin-stained waters)
Overwing: Peacock herl
Thread: Danville flat waxed nylon, white
Tier Comments: This is a very basic, old, standard pattern that is easy to tie, is productive, and is naturally weedless.

Prey Species: Atlantic Silverside
Fly Pattern: Gordo's Glass Minnow
Fly Type: Imitation

TIER: GORDON CHURCHILL

Hook: Gamakatsu Octopus hook, or similar short shank
Tail: Sparse white bucktail
Underwing: Peacock Flashabou and chartreuse Flashabou
Overwing: Olive bucktail/silver Krystal Flash
Head: Silver tinsel or Bill's Bodi-Braid
Eye: Small rattling doll eye or prism eye
Thread: 3/0 mono or white thread

Tying Instructions
1. Wrap the hook shank with thread as shown, and add a sparse underwing on the shank, slightly ahead of the hook point. This serves as the tail or belly.
2. Add a small clump of peacock Flashabou using the "double-back" method, just forward of the bucktail toward the hook eye. ("Double-back" means cutting the material to twice the length desired, and then tying it in at the halfway point, folding over [or doubling back] the second half over the first, and then securing with thread.)
3. On top and in front of the peacock Flashabou, add a layer of chartreuse Flashabou, again with the double-back method.
4. Add a sparse wing of olive bucktail on top and in front of the Flashabou body.
5. Build the head with silver tinsel or Bill's Bodi-Braid.
6. Finish off with a googly eye for rattle or a prismatic eye for profile, and whip-finish.

Tier Comments: This simple, small, and flashy fly is designed to imitate Atlantic silversides (aka glass minnows). The fly looks better in the water than the real thing!

Prey Species: Atlantic Silverside (also bay anchovy)
Fly Pattern: Atlantic Silverside
Fly Type: Imitation

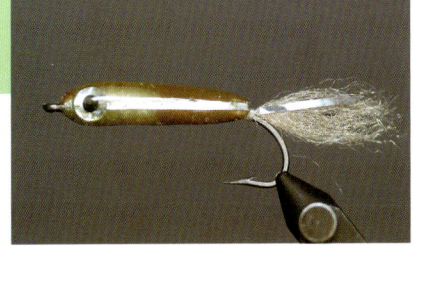

TIER: RON WINN

Hook: Mustad 34011, size 2
Tail: Tan macramé fibers
Body: Light tan to cream macramé fibers
Wing: Tan macramé fibers
Flash: Mylar tinsel
Eye: Stick-on eyes
Thread: 3/0 mono or white thread

Tier Comments: The body is coated with epoxy. This fly is obviously very durable, so it is a good choice for bluefish and Spanish mackerel. The hook shank can be wrapped with lead wire to make the fly sink deeper.

Prey Species: Atlantic Silverside
Fly Pattern: Bonito Deceiver
Fly Type: Imitation

TIER: DAVE SKOK

Hook: TMC 811S or other standard-length shank, sizes 1/0 to 4
Tail: Two thin white hackles (coated with a touch of Softex glue to past the bend) flanked by short white bucktail or calf tail
Body: Pearl or silver Bill's Bodi-Braid
Collar: Pearl Flashabou or UV Krystal Flash with sparse white bucktail or calf tail underneath, with darker bucktail over back
Eyes: 2½-inch EY prismatic

Prey Species: Silverside
Fly Pattern: Silverside Rapala
Fly Type: Imitation

TIER: GINGER ALLEN

Hook: Mustad 34011, size 1
Body: Pearl and silver medium Gudebrod body tubing, stuffed with white foam on top of hook shank, holographic silver flash along sides, coated with epoxy
Eyes: Silver 3D Mylar
Thread: Clear mono
Tier Comments: This fly's originator was Curtis Grant.

Prey Species: Silverside
Fly Pattern: Glenn's Glass Minnow
Fly Type: Impressionistic

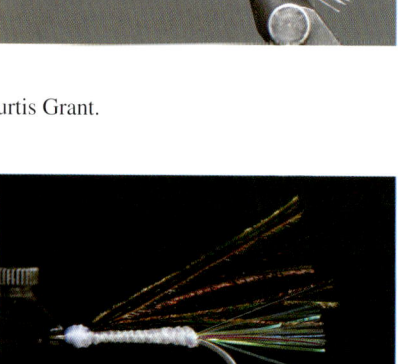

TIER: GLENN PITTARD

Hook: Mustad 34007, size 2
Eyes: Painted or stick-on (optional)
Tail: Pearl Flashabou
Wing: Peacock herl
Body: Mylar body braid
Thread: Danville flat waxed nylon, white

Prey Species: Silverside
Fly Pattern: Crystal Minnow
Fly Type: Impressionistic

TIER: GLENN PITTARD

Hook: Mustad 34007, size 2
Eyes: Stick-on molded eyes
Wing: White bucktail, over which is pearl and root beer Krystal Flash, over which is white Fishair colored with a permanent marker
Body: Pearl cactus chenille, back painted with a permanent marker
Thread: Danville flat waxed nylon, white
Tier Comments: This is a variation of a long-popular pattern with coloration added to match local species.

Prey Species: Silversides (and anchovies)
Fly Pattern: Chartreuse and White Clouser Minnow
Fly Type: Impressionistic

TIER: AARON ADAMS

Hook: Mustad 34007, size 1
Weight: Silver dumbbells, medium
Underwing: White bucktail
Overwing: Chartreuse bucktail over pearl Krystal Flash
Thread: Danville flat waxed nylon, chartreuse
Tier Comments: This standard pattern is perhaps one of the most-used patterns in saltwater fly fishing. This color combination can be used in many situations. I tend to use it when fishing in areas with silversides and anchovies.

Prey Species: Silverside
Fly Pattern: Fishair Silverside
Fly Type: Imitation

TIER: AARON ADAMS

Hook: Mustad 34007, size 2
Wing: Olive over white Fishair, tied in behind the hook eye
Stripe: Silver Flashabou
Eyes: $3/16$-inch hologram eyes
Overcoat: Silicone, two coats (apply the side stripe between coats)
Thread: Flat waxed nylon, olive

**Prey Species: Silversides
 (also anchovies)
Fly Pattern: Cactus Minnow
Fly Type: Impressionistic**

TIER: AARON ADAMS

Hook: Mustad 34007, size 1
Body: Pearl cactus chenille or estaz, tied in at hook bend, palmered forward to hook eye
Wing: White Kinky Fiber, pearl Flashabou
Thread: Flat waxed nylon, white
Tier Comments: I don't know the originator of this pattern, but variations on this theme have long been popular for imitations of anchovies and silversides. This pattern and the one below (Cactus Minnow Floater) can be good searching patterns in areas with anchovies and silversides.

**Prey Species: Silversides
 (also anchovies)
Fly Pattern: Cactus Minnow Floater
Fly Type: Impressionistic**

TIER: AARON ADAMS

Hook: Mustad 34007, size 1
Underbody: A strip of $1/8$-inch fly foam (same foam used for Gurglers), $1/4$-inch wide and the length of the hook shank. Tie in at the hook bend, and tie to the hook shank with widely spaced thread wraps.
Body: Pearl cactus chenille or estaz, tied in at hook bend, palmered forward to hook eye
Wing: White bucktail, pearl Flashabou
Thread: Flat waxed nylon, white
Tier Comments: This pattern is a variation of the Cactus Minnow modified to float or ride just subsurface. This is accomplished with the underbody of foam and bucktail instead of marabou for the wing.

**Prey Species: Silversides
(also anchovies)
Fly Pattern: Crazy Charlie
Fly Type: Impressionistic**

TIER: AARON ADAMS

Hook: Mustad 34007, size 4
Tail: Silver Mylar tips
Underbody: Silver Mylar, wrapped around hook shank
Overbody: 15-pound-test monofilament wrapped over Mylar
Wing: White calf tail
Thread: Flat waxed nylon, white
Tier Comments: This famous standard was created by Bob Nauheim. I think it's a great mimic of the small "glass minnows" (silversides and anchovies) that bonefish sometimes focus on as prey. The fly is good in any situation where small silversides and anchovies are the prey of choice. I prefer calf tail for the wing because it is more durable than the hackle tips used in the original fly.

**Prey Species: Silversides
Fly Pattern: Secret Silverside
Fly Type: Imitation**

TIER: JACK GARTSIDE

Hook: Daiichi 2546, Mustad 34007, or similar, sizes 2 to 1/0
Tailwing: Gartside's Secret Stuff (GSS)
Body and Wing: Pearl GSS picked out, combed back, and shaped to form silversides shape; overlaid with peacock GSS. Head cement applied to head area to harden material.
Eyes: Black on yellow; fabric paint applied with wooden kitchen match head
Thread: Danville 3/0, white
Author Comments: GSS is available directly from Jack Gartside's website, www.jackgartside.com.

CHAPTER 26

Herrings
Clupeidae

Prey Type: Baitfish
Primary Habitats: Open water, such as estuary, lagoon, and coastal habitats
Geographic Range: Throughout the tropics, subtropics, and warm-temperate regions
Comments: There are two dozen species of herrings in the regions covered in this book, most very similar in appearance. The species most commonly encountered by fly anglers are listed here. Coloration varies somewhat among species (e.g., green dorsal versus blue dorsal) but generally not so much that a couple patterns won't suffice. In fact, having flies of different sizes is probably more important, since you may encounter herrings from juvenile to adult, depending on season and location.

Habitat differences can cause color variation within a species as well; fish in clear or milky water tend to be more silver-backed, whereas fish in tannin-stained or brackish water tend to be dark-backed.

Herring seasonal migrations can be inshore-offshore as well as more "conventional" north-south. Herrings are schooling species with rapid growth rates and are important prey for most coastal gamefish. Red drum along the northern Gulf of Mexico coast, for example, feed heavily on menhaden in the fall. Herrings are also seasonally important prey for other gamefish. I've even seen bonefish join in feeding on schools of panicked herring on tropical islands.

Tarpon also feed heavily on herrings, sometimes pushing schools against shorelines in an all-out frenzy—in these cases, all that is needed is a White Deceiver. When living in the Virgin Islands, the only fly I used for tarpon was a Blueback Deceiver. This was, in part, because we didn't target tarpon but came upon them opportunistically. During these opportune times, the tarpon were usually feeding on herring. Despite the dominance of Keys-style flies for tarpon fishing, members of the herring family are probably at the top of the menu for tarpon during portions of the year.

Species: Scaled Sardine (aka whitebait, pilchard)

Harengula jaguana

Primary Habitats: Multiple open water habitats including beaches, bays, and lagoons
Geographic Range: New England to Florida, Gulf of Mexico to Brazil
Size Range: to 10 inches, but usually smaller
Comments: This is probably the most common herring species in coastal Florida waters.

Species: Spanish Sardine (aka cigar minnow)

Sardinella aurita

Primary Habitats: Multiple open water habitats; beach is the primary habitat.
Geographic Range: Gulf of Mexico to Caribbean
Size Range: to 10 inches, but generally smaller

Species: Alewife

Alosa pseudoharengus

Primary Habitats: Coastal rivers (spawning), estuaries, beaches
Geographic Range: New England to South Carolina
Size Range: to 15 inches, typically smaller except for fish in spawning runs
Comments: The alewife is identical to blueback herring, except it tends to have a greenish-hued back. It is able to tolerate lower salinity water than the blueback herring, so spawning runs tend to be farther upstream.

Herrings (Clupeidae)

Species: Menhaden (various species)

Brevoortia spp

Primary Habitats: Multiple open water habitats; beach is the primary habitat. They also occur in open waters of shallow bays and lagoons.
Geographic Range: New England to Florida, Gulf of Mexico
Size Range: to 12 to 14 inches
Comments: Juvenile menhaden live mostly in estuaries, whereas adults live in open ocean waters, except when they move near shore to spawn. Menhaden tend to be most abundant near shore areas during fall (warm-temperate) and late fall and winter (subtropical).

Species: Atlantic Thread Herring (aka threadfin, greenie, greenback)

Opisthonema oglinum

Primary Habitats: Multiple open water habitats; beach is the primary habitat. They also occur in shallow bays and lagoons and over deep grass beds.
Geographic Range: New England to Florida, Gulf of Mexico through Brazil
Size Range: to 12 inches, though generally smaller

Species: Redear Sardine

Harengula humeralis

Primary Habitats: Multiple open water habitats; beach is the primary habitat. They also occur in shallow bays and lagoons.
Geographic Range: Caribbean, south Florida, Bahamas
Size Range: to 8 inches
Comments: They are common in coastal bays and lagoons, especially with nutrient-rich water.

Species: Blueback Herring

Alosa aestivalis

Primary Habitats: Coastal rivers (spawning), estuaries, beaches
Geographic Range: New England to Northeast Florida
Size Range: to 15 inches, typically smaller except for fish in spawning runs
Comments: They are identical to alewife (above) except with a bluish-hued back. Blueback herring and alewife seasonally migrate offshore (winter) and inshore (warmer months).

BAITFISH

FLIES

Prey Species: Scaled Sardine and Other Herrings (Clupeidae)
Fly Pattern: Skok's Mushmouth Variant
Fly Type: Imitation

TIER: AARON ADAMS

Hook: Mustad 34007, size 1
Tail: Nylon hair, white
Body: Angel Hair, Wing N Flash, or similar, pearl
Eyes: Stick-on eyes
Thread: Danville flat waxed nylon, white
Tying Tips: After tying in the nylon hair, apply a liberal amount of Softex onto the nylon hair. While the nylon hair is still wet, tie in the body of Angel Hair reverse-style—first the bottom, then the top. Use your fingers to smooth the Angel Hair backwards, making sure some of the Softex sinks into the Angel Hair. This helps the fly maintain shape and increases durability. After applying the stick-on eyes, coat the head with a thin layer of Softex to help maintain fly shape. This pattern can also be tied entirely with white Slinky Fiber, in which case the nylon hair and Softex can be left out.
Tier Comments: This is a simplified version of Dave Skok's Mushmouth pattern, with a slightly higher profile than Dave's original. It is a quick and easy tie.

Prey Species: Pilchard (aka scaled sardine)
Fly Pattern: Mac Pilchard or Greenie
Fly Type: Imitation

TIER: RON WINN

Hook: Mustad 34007, sizes 1/0 to 4/0, bendback-style
Body: Light-colored macramé (fibers unwound from macramé cord) for underside of fly, darker macramé for upper side of fly, Krystal Flash
Eyes: Stick-on eyes
Weight: Lead wire wrapped around the hook shank
Thread: Monocord
Tier Comments: This fly is tied bendback-style, with all materials tied on the hook point side of the shank. Lead wire wrapped around the hook shank halfway to the bend helps the fly sink deeper and ensures that the fly swims upright.
This pattern of a deep-bodied baitfish is highly adaptive to the many baitfish with similar shapes and appropriate color variations. A small amount of silicone or Softex applied at the head is helpful for maintaining the shape of the fly.

Herring Flies

Prey Species: Atlantic Thread Herring
Fly Pattern: The Mushmouth
Fly Type: Imitation

TIER: DAVE SKOK

Hook: Mustad C68S SS or other short-shank hook, size 2/0
Tail: White or polar bear Super Hair, tapered and surrounded by metallic Flashabou, saturated with Softex or Soft Body (entire hook shank to past the bend)
Belly: Pearl or other light color Wing N Flash (tied reverse-style)
Back: Wing N Flash (tied reverse-style)—thread wraps and back material should have liberal dose of Softex or Soft Body
Eyes: Size 3.5 EY prismatic eye, epoxied
Thread: Clear mono, fine

Prey Species: Menhaden
Fly Pattern: Mega Mushy (adult menhaden)
Fly Type: Imitation

TIER: DAVE SKOK

Hook: Tiemco 600SP or other short-shank hook, size 6/0
Tail: White or polar bear Super Hair, tapered, surrounded by metallic Flashabou or Flashabou Mirage, saturated with Softex or Soft Body (entire hook shank to past the bend)
Belly: White or natural color blended Slinky Fiber or Mega Mushy material (tied reverse-style)
Back: Blended Slinky Fiber or Mega Mushy material (tied reverse-style)—thread wraps and back material should have liberal dose of Softex or Soft Body
Eyes: Size 8 MEY 3D prismatic eye, epoxied on top and bottom
Thread: Clear mono, fine
Tier Comments: To learn Steve Farrar's flash blending technique, go to the Atlantic Saltwater Flyrodders' Web site: www.aswf.org/saltwater_flies_for_web/steve_farrar/saltwater_flies_steve_flas.html.

Prey Species: Menhaden
Fly Pattern: Hollow Deceiver
 (medium-size menhaden)
Fly Type: Imitation

TIER: DAVE SKOK

Hook: Varivas 994S or other longish shank hook, size 3/0
Tail: Four white saddle hackles with a smaller grizzly saddle on each side
Body: Three progressively shorter 360-degree bunches of white bucktail tied hollow-style, with blue, green, and chartreuse flash at various intervals and holographic lavender body braid between each bundle of hair
Eyes: 1/4-inch Tab prismatic fly eyes or jungle cock eyes
Thread: 3/0 monocord, white

Prey Species: Herrings/sardines
Fly Pattern: White Beach Fly
 (also, mangrove minnow, white)
Fly Type: Imitation

TIER: DOUG HEDGES

Hook: Mustad 34007, size 4
Wing: White craft fur mixed with pearl flash
Head: White craft fur coated with Softex
Eyes: 3D prism eyes
Thread: Danville flat waxed nylon, white
Weedguard: 17-pound-test Hard Mason doubled monofilament

Prey Species: Herrings/sardines
Fly Pattern: Delta Dart Minnow
 (large or small versions)
Fly Type: Impressionistic

TIER: TOM BERRY

Hook: Eagle Claw 254, size 4/0 (large version); Mustad 34007, size 2/0, small version
Tail: Green Kinky Fiber, over green Krystal Flash, over yellow Kinky Fiber
Head: Clear plastic, folded and cut to shape, coated with epoxy
Body: Ice chenille (for large version) or ultra chenille (for small version), palmered over hook shank
Eyes: Molded eyes
Body Color: Permanent markers, color to suit
Thread: Danville flat waxed nylon, white

Herring Flies

Prey Species: Threadfin Herring
Fly Pattern: Thread Herring
Fly Type: Imitation

TIER: AARON ADAMS

Hook: Owner 5115-121, size 2/0
Wing: Kinky Fiber in order of tying—white, yellow, light blue, purple, black; pearl Flashabou after yellow and purple
Eyes: Stick-on, molded, or prismatic
Thread: Danville flat waxed nylon, white
Tier Comments: This fly has proven successful in areas where tarpon may be feeding on threadfin herring or other members of this family.

Prey Species: Sardine
Fly Pattern: Juvenile Sardine
Fly Type: Imitation

TIER: AARON ADAMS

Hook: Mustad 34007, size 1 or 1/0
Wing: White Fishair, over which is sparse chartreuse Fishair, topped by chartreuse Wing N Flash
Eyes: Stick-on prismatic
Overcoat: Silicone, smoothed backward from hook eye over body
Thread: Danville flat waxed nylon, white
Tier Comments: This fly imitates juveniles of some of the slender-bodied sardines.

Prey Species: Spanish Sardine
Fly Pattern: Spanish Sardine
Fly Type: Imitation

TIER: AARON ADAMS

Hook: Mustad 34007, size 1 or 1/0
Wing: In order of tying—white Fishair; white, chartreuse, aqua Kinky Fiber; pearl Flashabou tied in after white Kinky Fiber
Eyes: Stick-on prismatic
Overcoat: Silicone, smoothed backward from hook eye over body
Thread: Danville flat waxed nylon, white
Tier Comments: This fly has proven to be a successful imitation of Spanish sardines.

Prey Species: Sardine
Fly Pattern: Corsair Minnow
Fly Type: Imitation

TIER: AARON ADAMS

Hook: Mustad 34007, size 1 or 1/0
Wing: Olive bucktail over pearl Flashabou, over white bucktail (colors can be changed to match local species)
Body: Corsair tubing
Eyes: Stick-on prismatic
Overcoat: After eyes are put in place, coat Corsair body with Softex
Thread: Danville flat waxed nylon, white

Tying Instructions
1. Before tying the fly, cut the Corsair tubing to shape (front end blunt, back end tapered).
2. Run the thread through the Corsair tubing, and allow the tubing to rest on the shaft of the bobbin while the bucktail is tied in.
3. Tie in the bucktail and Flashabou on the top side of the hook shank. Leave the butt ends of the bucktail extending past the hook eye approximately $1/4$ inch.
4. Bend back the butt ends toward the hook bend, and slide the Corsair tubing onto the hook shank, with the blunt end just behind the hook eye. The butt ends help puff up the Corsair tubing, making a rounder head.
5. Tie down the Corsair tubing and then whip-finish.
6. After placing the stick-on eyes, apply a thin coat of Softex to the body.

Prey Species: Herrings
Fly Pattern: Buz's Snook Body Fly
Fly Type: Imitation

TIER: BUZ FENDER

Hook: Eagle Claw L253, size 1/0; Gamagatsu SC15, size 2/0
Body: Neer Hair or H_2O Fiber; green over white
Gill: Red body fur
Flash: Pearl Firefly (or Pearl Flashabou), tied at midbody, extending past tail
Eyes: 6-millimeter white or yellow solid plastic eyes
Thread: Danville flat waxed nylon (color to match); 3/0 monocord
Weedguard: #3 or #4 stainless steel wire; alteratively, 20-pound-test Mason monofilament
Tying Tips: Start toward the back of the hook shank and build the fly from the bottom up. Tie this fly with sparse amounts of material. Softex or silicone can be added on the head to help prevent fouling.
Tier Comments: When I first came up with this pattern, I used Aqua Fiber, which is no longer available, so now I use Neer Hair or H_2O Fiber. I like to use this fly along mangrove shorelines, primarily for snook. This fly is also good for spotted seatrout and redfish.

Herring Flies

Prey Species: Herrings
Fly Pattern: Buz's Snook Yak Fly
Fly Type: Imitation

TIER: BUZ FENDER

Hook: Eagle Claw L253, size 1/0; Gamagatsu SC15, size 2/0
Body: Chartreuse yak saltwater fibers, over Angel Hair, over white yak saltwater fibers
Gill: Red body fur
Cheek: Short and sparse white yak fibers and Angel Hair
Eyes: $1/4$-inch or $5/16$-inch holographic red, yellow, or mirage
Thread: Danville flat waxed nylon (color to match)
Weedguard: #3 or #4 stainless steel wire; alteratively, 20-pound-test Mason monofilament
Tier Comments: This fly works great in off-colored water. Other colors can be used for the topping to match local herrings. For the flash, I use yellow with a chartreuse-back fly, chartreuse with an olive-back fly.

Prey Species: Sardine
Fly Pattern: Polar Fiber Minnow
Fly Type: Imitation

TIER: GLENN PITTARD

Hook: Mustad 34007, size 1 or 2
Tail: White bucktail, white Kinky Fiber
Wing: White polar fiber
Eyes: Painted or stick-on
Thread: White

Tying Instructions
1. Tie in thread at hook bend.
2. At the hook bend and on top of the shank, tie in a small bunch of white bucktail followed by a small bunch of white Kinky Fiber and then a few strands of pearl Krystal Flash. At this point I like to tie another small bunch of white bucktail on top of the hook bend and over the previously tied in materials.
3. Add eight to ten strands of pearl Krystal Flash and bring the thread forward.
4. Just behind the hook eye, begin to tie in small clumps of polar fiber. Light wraps of the thread will help spread the material around the hook eye before pulling them down tight. Finish the body with a clump of dark green Angel Hair flash.
5. Whip-finish a head and coat with epoxy.
6. Paint on or use prism eyes and then coat with fingernail polish.

Prey Species: Pilchard
Fly Pattern: Pilchard
Fly Type: Imitation

TIER: CHRIS DEAN

Hook: Mustad 3407SS, size 3/0
Wing: Six white saddles hackles (4 inches long), three to each side, curving inward (Deceiver-style), tied in at midshank
Collar: White bucktail tied in just ahead of the wing; one yellow saddle hackle on top of the collar, tied in flat and curving down
Eyes: 8-millimeter doll eyes glued just in front of the collar with 30-minute epoxy
Throat: White bucktail tied in front of the eyes
Topping: Chartreuse ice Angel Hair (3-inch long) over white bucktail
Head: White thread
Thread: Flat waxed nylon, white
Tier Comments: This is a variation of a goggle-eye fly (aka Big-eye Scad) tied by Leo Dominguez. I kept the color scheme but changed the construction to give it a more pilchardlike shape. One of my customers caught a sailfish on this pattern while we were chumming with pilchards off Key West.

Prey Species: Herrings
Fly Pattern: blueback Deceiver
Fly Type: Imitation

TIER: AARON ADAMS

Hook: Owner 5311-121, size 2/0
Wing: Four white saddle hackles tied in at the hook bend, curving inward
Collar: White bucktail for belly and sides, blue bucktail for top, pearl Flashabou on sides
Eyes: Prismatic stick-on or doll eyes
Head: Softex from hook eye to just behind eyes
Thread: Flat waxed nylon, white
Tier Comments: This is merely a contrasting-color combination (mimics the countershading of many baitfish) of the standard Lefty's Deceiver. It has worked well for me when fishing for tarpon on Caribbean islands. Despite all the fantastic new flies out there, sometimes it's the old standards that perform best.

Prey Species: Herrings
Fly Pattern: Oscar's Blue Darter
Fly Type: Imitation

TIER: OSCAR FELIU

Hook: Mustad Signature C47S D, sizes 6 and 4
Underbody: Red or orange Puglisi fibers, cut short
Body: Puglisi fibers, very sparse—white for the belly, sides, and top; light brown or beige for midbody; blue Wing N Flash for the top
Eyes: 3D, affixed to the sea fibers with Super Glue
Thread: Danville A+, white
Finish: Coat head and eyes with epoxy

Prey Species: Threadfin Herring
Fly Pattern: Oscar's Threadfin
Fly Type: Imitation

TIER: OSCAR FELIU

Hook: Mustad S71S SS, size 3/0; VMC light wire, size 4/0; or Eagle Claw Black finish, size 5/0
Tail: Six or eight white saddle hackles, 2 to 3 inches in length; six strands of pearlescent Flashabou
Underbody: White Artic fox tail hair sparsely layered with strands of Wing N Flash
Body: White Puglisi fibers, extending at least an inch beyond the hook bend
Top: Chartreuse Puglisi fibers mixed with Wing N Flash fibers, extending an inch beyond the hook bend
Eyes: 7-millimeter 3D eyes affixed to clear plastic triangles, tied in with thread
Thread: Danville A+, white (I use white thread colored with permanent markers)
Finish: A coat of fast-drying epoxy on the head and eyes
Tier Comments: I prefer light wire hooks, and on occasion I'll use a 7/0 circle hook. Body fibers must be trimmed to a taper.

Prey Species: Herrings
Fly Pattern: Oscar's Herring
Fly Type: Imitation

TIER: OSCAR FELIU

Hook: Mustad S71S SS, size 1 or 1/0; VMC light wire, size 1/0; or Eagle Claw Black finish, size 1/0
Tail: Six white saddle hackles; six strands of pearlescent Flashabou
Underbody: White Artic fox tail hair sparsely layered with pearl Wing N Flash
Body: White Puglisi fibers

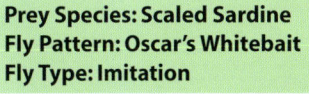

Top: Blue Puglisi sea fibers mixed with blue Wing N Flash
Eyes: 7-millimeter 3D eyes affixed to clear plastic triangles, tied in with thread
Thread: Danville A+, white
Finish: A coat of fast drying epoxy on the head and eyes
Tier Comments: This is a smaller, slimmed-down version of Oscar's Threadfin. The chartreuse midbody stripe is made with permanent markers.

Prey Species: Herrings
Fly Pattern: Oscar's Sardine
Fly Type: Imitation

TIER: OSCAR FELIU

Hook: Mustad S71S SS, size 1 or 1/0; VMC light wire, size 1/0; or Eagle Claw black finish, size 1/0
Tail: Six white saddle hackles
Underbody: White Artic fox tail hair sparsely layered with pearl Wing N Flash
Body: White Puglisi fibers
Top: Blue Puglisi fibers, over light blue Kinky Fiber, over blue Wing N Flash
Eyes: 7-millimeter 3D eyes affixed to clear plastic triangles, tied in with thread
Thread: Danville A+, white
Finish: A coat of fast-drying epoxy on the head and eyes
Tier Comments: This is a smaller, slimmed-down version of Oscar's Threadfin.

Prey Species: Scaled Sardine
Fly Pattern: Oscar's Whitebait
Fly Type: Imitation

TIER: OSCAR FELIU

Hook: Light wire circle, size 3/0 or 4/0
Tail: Four white saddle hackles, four strands of pearl Flashabou
Skirt: A clump of white calf tail to flank the saddle hackles
Body: White Puglisi fibers mixed with Wing N Flash 
Top: Your choice of steel-blue, olive, or beige fibers (bottom photo) or bucktail (top photo)
Eyes: 7-millimeter 3D eyes affixed to clear plastic triangles, tied in with thread
Thread: Danville A+, white; or 3/0 monocord
Tier Comments: I like to tie this fly in a Deceiver fashion about 3 to 4 inches in total length. My choice of hook is a circle light wire 3/0 or 4/0. (Circle hooks are much smaller than normal hooks of the same size.)

Herring Flies

Prey Species: Scaled Sardine
Fly Pattern: Bay Whistler
Fly Type: Impressionistic

TIER: CRAIG SMOTHERS

Hook: Mustad 34007, sizes 2 or 4
Tail: Four to six splayed white or chartreuse grizzly neck feathers, three to four strands of opal Flashabou Mirage
Body: White or light dun body fur
Eyes: Mini lead eyes
Thread: Flymaster 6/0, white or chartreuse
Tier Comments: This is a quick and easy fly to tie, originated by Capt. Keith Tennent. Body fur is one of the few synthetics I'm happy to use. This is a tough version of a Seaducer.

Prey Species: Scaled Sardine
Fly Pattern: Night Deceiver
Fly Type: Impressionistic

TIER: CRAIG SMOTHERS

Hook: Tiemco 811S, size 1/0
Tail: Four to eight matched white neck feathers, four to six strands of opal Flashabou accent
Low Body: White bucktail, ten strands of opal Mirage accent
Mid Body: Three strands of white glow-in-the-dark Flashabou, two strands of black Krystal Flash
Top Body: Gray bucktail, eight strands of lavender Krystal Flash, eight strands of gray Fire Fly Tye
Cheek: Mallard flake feather
Throat: Red rabbit hair
Eyes: Silver prismatic 5-millimeter decal eyes (overcoat with epoxy)
Thread: Flymaster 6/0, white
Tier Comments: This is my best snook/baby tarpon fly (10 to 30 pounds).

Prey Species: Blueback Herring
Fly Pattern: Blueback Herring
Fly Type: Imitation

TIER: JACK GARTSIDE

Hook: Daiichi 2546, Mustad 34007, or similar, sizes 1 to 1/0
Tailwing: Black, over blue, over white sheep hair
FishHead: 1/2-inch white Corsair tubing, colored blue on top and along lateral line with water-resistant olive marker
Thread: Danville 6/0, white

Prey Species: Herrings
Fly Pattern: Slinky Hi-Tie
Fly Type: Impressionistic

TIER: AARON ADAMS

Hook: Owner, SSW Bait Hook, #5311-121, size 2/0
Wing: Slinky Fiber (aka Kinky Fiber) of contrasting colors—lighter color on the bottom, darker color on top
Eyes: 3/8-inch prismatic stick-on
Thread: Danville flat waxed nylon, color to match wing

Tying Instructions
1. All materials are tied in on the top of the hook shank. Pull a small (pencil-size or smaller), full-length clump of Slinky Fiber from the main bunch.
2. Starting at the hook bend, tie in the clump parallel to the hook shank, with one end extending a few inches off the back and the longer end extending past the hook eye.
3. After securing with a few thread wraps, fold the forward-facing fibers back over the tie-in spot so they extend rearward. Secure the fiber clump with a few thread wraps immediately in front of the folded over fibers. This should keep the fibers pointing upwards and slightly back over the hook bend.
4. Repeat this process, changing to the darker contrasting color about halfway along the hook shank.
5. Whip-finish just behind the hook eye, trim the thread, and coat head with nail polish or epoxy.
6. Trim body to shape.
7. Place a small drop of Goop (or similar product) on the fly where the eyes will go, and press an eye onto each side of the body.

Tier Comments: These flies are lightweight, easy to cast, and provide a good profile, making them easy for the fish to see. This pattern is my favorite for tarpon, in a variety of colors. Productive colors are blue and white, green and yellow, black and red, black and purple. Hi-tie-style flies are popular in many situations for many gamefish. My first use of this pattern for tarpon was inspired by the Puglisi Peanut Bunker, but I find this pattern a considerably faster and easier tie.

Herring Flies

CHAPTER 27

Needlefishes, Halfbeaks, and Ladyfish

Belonidae, Exocoetidae, and Elopidae

Prey Type: Baitfish
Primary Habitats: Mostly shallow areas, including estuaries, lagoons, and beaches; needlefish and halfbeaks—coastal areas (including bays, lagoons, and beaches) and deeper waters offshore; ladyfish—coastal areas (including bays, lagoons, and beaches)
Geographic Range: Primarily subtropical and tropical regions, but seasonally present in some warm-temperate areas

NEEDLEFISH

Species: Needlefishes

Strongylura spp

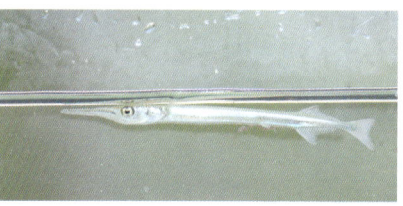

Many species occur in the regions covered in this book, and all are very similar in appearance. Their coloration varies from electric blue to aqua-green, with hints of chartreuse. In general, the clearer the water the more iridescent their coloration. A redfin needlefish is shown in these photos. Since it's difficult to capture the iridescence in a full-length photograph, I include close-ups of the head and midbody to capture some of this coloration. The middle photo on the right shows the typical orientation of needlefish to the water surface.

Primary Habitats: Shallow-waters, such as estuaries, lagoons, bays, and coastal waters
Geographic Range: Subtropical and tropical habitats, but also warm-temperate areas in summer
Comments: Needlefish live at or very near the water surface (note the orientation and position of the fish in the photograph) and move slowly or not at all unless chasing prey or being chased. They often greyhound across the water surface when pursuing prey, the theory being that they are able to move rapidly and more stealthily approach their prey (if they are out of the water, they can't be seen). In contrast, to escape predators, they often tail-walk across the water—the lower lobe of their tail fin is larger than the top lobe, which they use like a mini-outboard.

Although I have seen tarpon and snook eat needlefish, barracuda and other needlefish are probably their main predators, so it's a good practice to use wire when fishing needlefish flies.

HALFBEAKS AND FLYINGFISHES

Family: Exocoetidae (halfbeaks and flyingfishes)
Primary Habitats: Coastal areas (including bays, lagoons and beaches) and deeper waters offshore
Geographic Range: Primarily subtropical and tropical regions, but present in some warm-temperate areas in summer

Species: Balao

Hemiramphus balao

Primary Habitats: Coastal areas, primarily marine, open waters
Geographic Range: warm-temperate (summer), subtropical, and tropical areas
Size Range: to 16 inches, usually smaller
Comments: Balao is nearly identical in appearance and size to Ballyhoo *(Hemiramphus brasiliensis)* and Halfbeak *(Hyporhamphus unifasciatus)*. These species live very near the water surface. When chased by predators, they often tail-walk across the water—the lower lobe of their tail fin is larger than the top lobe, which they use like a mini-outboard. Although they occur into the warm-temperate region, they are most common in the tropics and southern subtropics. They are eaten by most fish-eating (piscivorous) gamefish in these regions.

Species: Hardhead Halfbeak

Chriodorus atherinoides

Primary Habitats: Coastal areas, primarily marine, usually over seagrass
Geographic Range: warm-temperate (summer), subtropical, and tropical areas
Size Range: to 10 inches, usually smaller
Comments: This species is usually mistaken for a giant silverside because they lack the beaklike extension, so oversized silverside patterns are effective. They swim in surface waters over shallow seagrass beds near shore. Coloration of the back can vary from pale silvery-tan (shown here) to olive, with the belly always pale below.

UPPER WATER PREY FISH

Family: Elopidae (Ladyfish)
Primary Habitats: Coastal areas, including bays, lagoons, and beaches
Geographic Range: Primarily subtropical and tropical regions, but seasonally present in some warm-temperate areas

Species: Ladyfish

Elops saurus

Primary Habitats: Coastal areas, including bays, lagoons, and beaches, primarily estuarine
Geographic Range: warm-temperate (summer), subtropical, and tropical areas
Size Range: to 36 inches, usually smaller
Comments: Ladyfish, especially smaller ones, are eaten by numerous gamefish, but especially tarpon. They move fast when feeding or being chased but will also rest, hovering in midwater.

FLIES

Prey Species: Needlefishes
Fly Pattern: Nylon Hair Needlefish, short
Fly Type: Impressionistic

TIER: AARON ADAMS

Hook: Mustad 34007, size 2/0
Tail: Nylon hair—chartreuse, over medium blue, over light blue, over white
Body: Palmered chartreuse hackle
Eyes: Doll eyes, glued on with Goop or similar
Head: Thread built up to size to accommodate eyes, coated with epoxy after eyes attached
Thread: Danville flat waxed nylon, chartreuse
Tier Comments: This is a very simple, lightweight, easy-to-cast, durable, and effective fly to tie.

Prey Species: Needlefishes
Fly Pattern: Nylon Hair Needlefish, long
Fly Type: Impressionistic

TIER: AARON ADAMS

Hook: Mustad 34007, size 2/0 or 3/0
Tail: Chartreuse nylon hair (aka Ultra Hair), over thin pearl Flashabou, over white nylon hair
Eyes: $3/8$-inch yellow prismatic stick-on
Head: Thread built up to taper, coated with epoxy after eyes attached
Thread: Danville flat waxed nylon, chartreuse
Tier Comments: I like to place the eyes at the hook bend and apply a coat of epoxy to just behind the eyes. This helps keep the nylon hair from wrapping around the hook bend.

Needlefish, Halfbeaks, and Ladyfish Flies

Prey Species: Needlefishes
Fly Pattern: Braided Needlefish Fly
Fly Type: Impressionistic

TIER: CHRIS DEAN

Hook: Mustad 34011, size 2/0
Tail: Chartreuse nylon braided, 10 inches long
Head: Chartreuse thread built up at the bend, covered with 30-minute epoxy
Eyes: Painted on, black over white
Thread: Flat waxed nylon, chartreuse
Tying Tip: Secure the braid at the tail with 12-pound-test monofilament and epoxy over the wraps.
Tier Comments: I started tying this variation of a fly tied by Pedro Arellano around 1986. I added the painted eyes and epoxied the body for durability. Originally, I tied the fly with Fishair, but now I tie with nylon because it's available and easier to work with. The important thing about the fly is to make it long. This is the best barracuda fly that I've used. You need to make long casts and strip fast for the fly to be most effective.

Prey Species: Halfbeaks
Fly Pattern: Nylon Hair Halfbeak
Fly Type: Imitation

TIER: AARON ADAMS

Hook: Mustad 34007, size 2/0 or 3/0
Tail: Blue-gray nylon hair (aka Ultra Hair), over white nylon hair, over thin pearl Flashabou
Eyes: $^5/_{16}$-inch silver hologram stick-on
Head: Thread built up to taper, end colored red with permanent marker, coated with epoxy after eyes attached
Thread: Danville flat waxed nylon, white
Tier Comments: I like to place the eyes at the hook bend and use epoxy to coat to just behind the eyes. This helps to keep the nylon hair from wrapping around the hook bend.

Prey Species: Ladyfish
Fly Pattern: Oscar's Ladyfish (Homosassa Deceiver)
Fly Type: Imitation

TIER: OSCAR FELIU

Hook: Mustad 34007, size 7/0 or 34011, size 5/0 (you may use two 3/0 hooks in tandem)
Tail: Eight to ten white saddle hackles, 6 inches to 7 inches in length, mixed with six strands of Flashabou
Skirt: Two clumps of 3-inch long calf tail hair flanking the saddle hackles
Underbody: Sparse bands of Artic fox white tail hair intermixed with Wing N Flash (repeat process several times to achieve the body mass desired)
Body: White Puglisi fibers to cover all the belly of the fly and about 3 inches beyond the hook bend
Top: Twelve blue Flashabou fibers veiled by sparse Puglisi fibers and topped with blue bucktail
Eyes: 3/8-inch or 1/2-inch 3D eyes affixed to clear plastic, attached with thread to the head
Thread: Danville A+, white
Finish: Fast-drying epoxy to cover the head and affixed eyes
Tier Comments: The Homosassa Deceiver was the first in a series of Deceivers I developed. It quickly became a favorite of several avid fly fishers in the Crystal River–Homosassa area. The colors and sizes changed according to which gamefish we were pursuing. The most popular of all was one that I tied for Capt. Matt Fleming. This fly was quite large, about 6 inches in length, and white and bright orange in color. Matt requested that I add more saddle hackles to create more action. I did, and on the water the fly took on a whole different look. When the fly first made contact with the water, it looked like a drowning chicken, so I renamed it Matt's Poultry. In spite of the funny name, it caught a lot of tarpon. As Matt and I discovered that tarpon have quite an appetite for ladyfish, we modified the pattern to imitate ladyfish.

CHAPTER 28

Mullets
Mugilidae

Prey Type: Baitfish
Primary Habitats: Shallow waters, such as estuaries, lagoons, bays, and along coastal shorelines
Geographic Range: Warm-temperate, subtropical, and tropical regions
Comments: Adult mullet are present year-round in the subtropics and tropics. Juvenile mullet (those most often eaten by gamefish) are most common in estuaries in all regions from summer through fall. In some regions they undergo coastal migrations: Along the southeastern U.S. coast, for example, juvenile mullet (primarily white mullet) migrate southward from warm-temperate estuaries in the fall. These migrating fish are fed upon by most coastal gamefish, including tarpon, snook, cobia, ladyfish, jacks, red drum, and barracuda, among others.

Most mullet grow large as adults, but it is the juvenile sizes that are most eaten by gamefish. Keep this in mind when tying mullet flies.

Mullet occur throughout the water column in shallow coastal habitats but tend to head for the water surface when being chased by gamefish, so most mullet imitations are unweighted and are fished near the surface.

Species: Striped (aka Black) Mullet

Mugil cephalis

Primary Habitats: Shallow coastal bays and lagoons, enters rivers, spawns in large schools offshore in winter
Geographic Range: New England to Florida, Gulf of Mexico, Brazil, absent from Caribbean
Size Range: to 30 inches

Species: White Mullet

Mugil curema

Primary Habitats: Shallow coastal bays and lagoons, enters rivers, large migratory schools in fall along the eastern coast
Geographic Range: New England to Florida, Gulf of Mexico and Caribbean
Size Range: to 15 inches

Species: Fantail Mullet

Mugil gyrans

Primary Habitats: Shallow coastal bays and lagoons, beaches, usually clear water
Geographic Range: Florida, Gulf of Mexico, Caribbean
Size Range: to 18 inches

Species: Liza

Mugil liza

Primary Habitats: Shallow coastal bays and lagoons, enters rivers
Geographic Range: Caribbean, including Florida and Bahamas (similar in appearance to striped mullet, and replaces striped mullet in the Caribbean)
Size Range: to 24 inches

This is the appearance of most junenile mullet (approximately 1–2 inches in length) found in early spring in marsh, mangrove, and other shallow protected habitats.

Mullets (Mugilidae)

FLIES

**Prey Species: Mullet
 (juvenile, aka finger mullet)
Fly Pattern: Gurgler
Fly Type: Impressionistic**

TIER: AARON ADAMS

Hook: Mustad 34007, size 1
Tail: White bucktail or Kinky Fiber under pearl Flashabou
Body: Palmered natural grizzly or white hackle
Back: $1/8$-inch white fly foam (thin)
Thread: Danville flat waxed nylon, white
Tier Comments: This pattern was originated by Jack Gartside and has proven effective for many species of gamefish in many locations. I've found Gurglers to be highly effective on shallow grass flats where red drum, spotted seatrout, and snook are feeding on finger mullet in late summer and fall. It's quite a sight to see red drum, with their subterminal mouth, eat a fly on the surface. I have also been told that bonefish will strike Gurglers on Los Roques.

**Prey Species: Mullet
 (aka finger mullet)
Fly Pattern: Phat Phoam Gurgler
Fly Type: Impressionistic**

TIER: AARON ADAMS

Hook: Mustad 34007, size 1
Tail: White Kinky Fiber under pearl Flashabou
Body: Palmered natural grizzly or white hackle
Back: $1/4$-inch white foam
Thread: Danville flat waxed nylon, white
Tier Comments: Unlike Gartside's original Gurgler, there is no underbody of foam tied on this pattern because none is needed. A rectangle of foam is cut to match the length of the hook shank, and then one end is cut to a tapered point. This tapered end is tied in at the hook bend after tying in the tail. If a weedguard is desired, tie it in behind the hook eye before tying down the front end of the foam. The Phat Phoam Gurgler is as easy to cast as Gartside's original Gurgler and gives as good a "pop" as the tough-to-cast hard-bodied poppers.

Prey Species: Mullet
Fly Pattern: Flexi-Mullet
Fly Type: Impressionistic

TIER: AARON ADAMS

Hook: Mustad 34007, sizes 1 to 2/0
Tail: Slender white hackle or white ostrich herl, over which is silver Flashabou, outside which is 1 slender grizzly hackle per side
Head: Pearl flexi-cord cone
Body: Flashabou tied in front of the flexicord cone, trailing back, pearl on the bottom half, darker color on the top half
Rattle: This is optional but adds another fishy component to the fly.
Thread: Danville flat waxed nylon, white

Tying Instructions
1. At the hook bend, tie in hackle tips and flash for tail, whip-finish, and trim thread.
2. If you are going to tie in a rattle, do so now on the middle of the hook shank.
3. Cut a length of flexi-cord the same length as the hook shank.
4. Pass the flexi-cord over the hook shank so one end is over the hook bend, the other over the hook eye.
5. Attach the thread to the shank just behind the hook eye, and tie down the forward end of the flexi-cord.
6. Fold the rear end of the flexi-cord forward (turning it inside-out), and tie it in at the same point as above (this should result in a flexi-cord cone, with the narrow end forward).
7. Tie in the Flashabou at the same point as above—dark above, light below—using multiple small clumps. The Flashabou should extend to approximately halfway along the length of the hackle tips.
8. Use your fingers to hold the tips of the Flashabou near the hook bend while using a bodkin to spread Softex over the head—be sure to apply enough Softex to soak the Flashabou to the flexi-cord cone.
9. I find it helpful to use a clothespin to hold the tail-end of the Flashabou in place while the Softex dries.

Tier Comments: This is a modification of a pattern originally shown to me by Jerry Goldsmith a few years ago. This fly has fantastic action when tied on the tippet with a loop knot. It can be tied relatively small or larger.

Prey Species: Mullet
Fly Pattern: Sea Trouter
Fly Type: Imitation

TIER: KEN BAY

Hook: Mustad 34007, size 1/0
Wing: White bucktail, 4 to 5 inches in length, grizzly hackle on each side
Overwing: Two dark gray hackles, tied flat
Head: Clear silicone sprinkled with silver glitter
Eyes: Gold and black stick-on
Thread: White nylon
Tier Comments: Joe Brooks's book *Salt Water Fly Fishing* has more references to Dick Splaine than any other fisherman, and his Squetauger caught my interest. This interest was fostered during a phone call with Ed Mitchell, who asked me about this pattern. When I first made this fly, I attempted to faithfully follow Joe Brooks's description, and I sent my flies to trout fishermen I knew. A local guide came to see me to pick up more flies and grabbed my grizzly-wing variant. I took the hint and continue to use grizzly hackle.

Prey Species: Mullet
Fly Pattern: Mullet Deceiver
Fly Type: Imitation

TIER: GLENN PITTARD

Hook: Mustad 34007, sizes 1 to 1/0
Tail: White saddle hackles, outside of which are grizzly hackles, one on each side
Collar: White bucktail with pearl Flashabou under gray bucktail
Eyes: Stick-on prism
Thread: White nylon
Tier Comments: I call this pattern a beach mullet because I enjoy fishing these at night during summer. I often tie this fly heavily dressed with a few wraps of lead wire around the hook shank to help the fly sink in the swiftly moving water in the inlets. I also like this pattern tied all white with a red head.

Prey Species: Mullet
Fly Pattern: Polar Fiber Mullet
Fly Type: Imitation

TIER: RON WINN

Hook: Mustad 34007, sizes 1 to 2/0; Owner Aki 5370-111, size 1/0
Overwing: Dark Angel Hair
Underwing: White polar fiber, with pearl or purple Angel Hair
Head Color: Red or purple polar fiber, palmered
Eyes: 3D plastic, attached with superglue
Thread: White nylon or monofilament
Tying Instructions
1. Tie the first few clumps of polar fiber atop the hook to form the tail.
2. Form the head by cutting a $1/4$-inch x $3/8$-inch strip of polar fiber, including the backing, attaching one end immediately in front of the tail clumps, and palmering forward. Be careful to stroke the fibers rearward as you palmer.
3. Add flash overwing and attach the eyes. Add silicone or Softex to the head to help maintain shape.

Tier Comments: Tied on a circle hook, the fly is nearly snag-proof and is great for casting around rocks and docks.

Prey Species: Mullet
Fly Pattern: Mac Mullet
Fly Type: Imitation

TIER: RON WINN

Hook: Mustad 34007, sizes 2 to 4/0; Eagle Claw D067F, size 2/0
Overwing: Dark gray brushed out macramé cord
Underwing: Pearl Flashabou, white brushed out macramé cord
Coating: Thin layer of clear silicone
Eyes: $7 1/2$ millimeter hard plastic, attached with Goop
Thread: White nylon or monofilament
Tying Instructions
1. Attach three consecutive small clumps of brushed out polycord, being careful to taper ends before tying down.
2. Attach flash, followed by collar of poly on each side of the head.
3. Head is prepared much like wool—skewer each clump (no more than three) to head.
4. Trim to shape, and apply silicone to head.
5. After silicone dries, attach eyes with Goop.

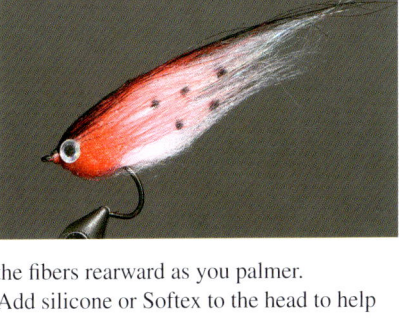

Prey Species: Mullet
Fly Pattern: Deer-hair Mullet
Fly Type: Imitation

TIER: DOUG HEDGES

Hook: Mustad 34007, size 1
Wing: White rabbit strip
Head: Stacked white and olive deer belly hair
Eyes: Medium dumbbell eyes
Thread: Monocord
Tier Comments: Tie in 17-pound-test Hard Mason antifoul loop at rear of hook and glue it to the rabbit strip tail.

Prey Species: Fantail Mullet
Fly Pattern: Fantail Mullet Deceiver
Fly Type: Impressionistic

TIER: GINGER ALLEN

Hook: Mustad 34007, size 1/0
Tail: White deer hair (antifouling), four white saddle hackle, covered by two whiting white/black furnace hen saddle, silver Krystal Flash
Body: Gudebrod silver Mylar HT braid
Shoulders: White deer hair
Wing: Grey deer hair, silver Krystal Flash, six to eight peacock herl
Chin: Red Flashabou
Eyes: Silver Mylar, head coated with epoxy
Thread: Gudebrod G, black
Weedguard: Wire leader
Tier Comments: The pattern originator is Lefty Kreh.

Prey Species: Striped Mullet
Fly Pattern: Striped Mullet Streamer
Fly Type: Impressionistic

TIER: GINGER ALLEN

Hook: Mustad C71S, size 1/0
Tail: Grizzly marabou, silver holographic flash
Body: Gudebrod silver holographic HT braid
Wing: White bucktail topped with four grey saddle hackle, covered by two grey grizzly saddle hackle
Chin: Red marabou
Head: Black thread coated with epoxy
Eyes: Silver holographic
Thread: Gudebrod 3/0, turquoise
Weedguard: Wire leader

Prey Species: Striped Mullet
Fly Pattern: Striped Mullet Seaducer
Fly Type: Impressionistic

TIER: GINGER ALLEN

Hook: Mustad 34007, size 2/0
Tail: Grey bucktail, silver holographic flash, 6 grizzly neck hackles splayed out, purple Krystal Flash
Body: Eight to ten grizzly saddle hackles palmered
Head: Red thread
Thread: Gudebrod G, red
Tier Comments: Originated by Homer Rhodes

Prey Species: Striped Mullet
Fly Pattern: Popovics's Siliclone
Fly Type: Imitation

TIER: DAVE SKOK

Hook: Varivas 990S or other wide-gap hook, size 3/0
Tail: Two collars of white ostrich bucktail surrounded by holographic silver Sparkleflash
Collar/Head: Pale blue sheep's fleece spun, combed and trimmed to shape
Eyes: Silver 3EY prismatic
Tier Comments: After trimming, the head is coated with two coats of clear silicone caulking. Pearl and silver glitter is applied between coats along with a prismatic eye. A finished appearance is made by smoothing the still wet silicone with Kodak Photo-Flo 200 solution or soapy water.

Prey Species: Mullet
Fly Pattern: Jerry's Mullet
Fly Type: Impressionistic

TIER: JERRY GOLDSMITH

Hook: Mustad 34007, size 1/0 or 2/0
Wing: 2 pair white saddle hackles, 1 pair gray saddle hackles, all hackle turned out; pearl Flashabou
Body: Pearl cactus chenille under palmered gray hackle
Eyes: Stick-on molded plastic or doll eyes

Mullet Flies

Prey Species: Juvenile White or Fantail Mullet (aka finger mullet)
Fly Pattern: Silicone Finger Mullet
Fly Type: Imitation

TIER: AARON ADAMS

Hook: Mustad 34007, size 1 or 1/0
Underbody: Chartreuse Fishair
Outerbody: White polar fiber, pearl Flashabou
Head: White polar fiber spun like wool and trimmed to shape
Overcoat: Silicone, brushed back from the hook eye, yellow spot added with permanent marker
Eyes: Stick-on molded plastic
Tier Comments: This fly holds air, so it stays just under the surface, just like its inspiration, Popovics's Siliclone. Tied to the tippet with a loop knot, the fly darts back and forth between strips. This fly is pretty specific to the late summer and fall when juvenile mullet are abundant.

Prey Species: Juvenile Mullet (aka finger mullet)
Fly Pattern: Marabou Muddler (short version)
Fly Type: Impressionistic

TIER: AARON ADAMS

Hook: Mustad 34007, size 1 or 1/0
Wing: White marabou, palmered from hook bend halfway up hook shank, over which is pearl Flashabou
Head: White bucktail, spun and packed
Weedguard: If desired, 30-pound-test monofilament
Tier Comments: This fly is simple and easy to tie, and it catches fish. Tied with a loop knot, the fly wobbles back and forth between strips, which is when fish often strike it. This short version is tied with only a marabou tail. The long version (see below) includes a hackle tail for stability.

Prey Species: Juvenile Mullet (aka finger mullet)
Fly Pattern: Marabou Muddler (long version)
Fly Type: Impressionistic

TIER: AARON ADAMS

Hook: Mustad 34007, size 1/0 or 2/0
Underwing: 6 to 8 white hackle tips, over which is pearl Flashabou

Wing: White marabou, palmered from hook bend, halfway up hook shank
Head: White bucktail, spun and packed
Weedguard: If desired, 30-pound-test monofilament
Tier Comments: The white hackle tips are just enough to reduce fouling by the marabou.

Prey Species: Mullet
Fly Pattern: Whistler
Fly Type: Impressionistic

TIER: GLENN PITTARD

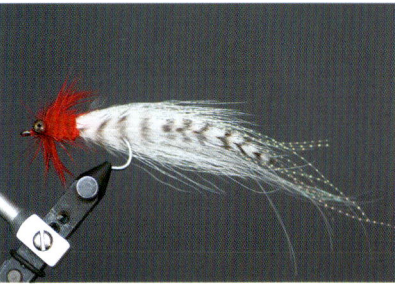

Hook: Mustad 34007, size 1
Eyes: Large bead chain
Wing: Bucktail, over which is grizzly saddle hackle, over which is pearl Krystal Flash
Body: Chenille
Head: Palmered hackle to match body
Thread: Danville flat waxed nylon, black

Tying Instructions
1. Start by tying in thread just forward of the hook point.
2. Place a clump of bucktail on top of the shank and tie in.
3. Tie in another clump of bucktail underneath the shank.
4. Tie in a pair of grizzly saddle hackles on each side of the wing.
5. Bring the thread forward and tie in eight to twelve strands of pearl Flashabou.
6. Tie in a length of chenille near the hook bend and make several wraps forward.
7. Just behind the hook eye, tie in a pair of large bead chain eyes, making several figure-eight wraps.
8. Tie in a grizzly hackle immediately behind the eyes, palmer it and make several wraps in front of and behind the eyes. Tie it off just in front of the bead chain eyes and whip-finish.

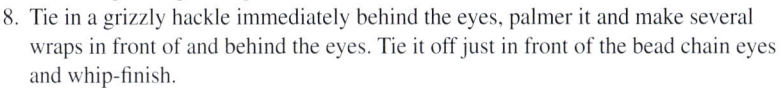

Tier Comments: This can be tied in any color combination, but my favorites are the three shown here. I like to use the black version at night fishing for snook in fast-moving water, and the other colors in conditions with more light. I also like it tied full.

Mullet Flies 177

Prey Species: Mullet
Fly Pattern: Hackle Muddler
Fly Type: Impressionistic

TIER: AARON ADAMS

Hook: Mustad 34007, size 2/0
Wing: Four natural grizzly hackle, over pearl Flashabou, over twelve natural white hackle, over white bucktail
Collar: Bucktail (white on bottom, gray on top)
Head: Spun bucktail, white on bottom, gray on top, trimmed to shape
Eyes: Large bead chain (optional)
Tier Comments: Because of the use of bucktail for the head and hackle for a tail, this fly should be cast with a 10-weight rod. It's a little heavy when wet, but it's a successful pattern and worth the effort for large fish. It really pushes a lot of water, and the combination of the large head and long, thin hackle makes the fly wobble when tied to the tippet with a loop knot.

Prey Species: Mullet
Fly Pattern: Oscar's Little Mullet
Fly Type: Imitation

TIER: OSCAR FELIU

Hook: Mustad C70SD, sizes 6, 4, and 2
Tail: 4 to 6 saddle hackles in a variety of colors
Body: Artic fox tail sparsely layered with Wing N Flash; white fox tail fibers for the belly and grey for the top; Puglisi sea fibers for a sparse veil to cover the body, which is trimmed to a taper
Head: 3D eyes affixed to clear triangular pieces of plastic, tied on with thread
Thread: Danville A+, white
Finish: Permanent markers to draw features such as gills; coat eyes and head with fast-drying epoxy
Tier Comments: This is a Deceiver-style fly with subsurface action. Small juvenile mullets are a staple diet of many inshore predators. This fly I tie with or without feathers for the tail. Without feathers, fishing friends and I have come to know as a "body fly." My favorite tail colors are white and grey with some strands of pearl flashabou. You may choose to use other flashy fibers such as Krystal Flash.

Prey Species: Mullet
Fly Pattern: Steve's Snook Fly (black)
Fly Type: Impressionistic

TIER: STEVE VENINI

Hook: Mustad 34007, size 2/0
Wing: Black marabou, over which is black holographic Flashabou
Collar: Black bucktail
Head: Spun black bucktail, spun red bucktail, trimmed to shape
Eyes: $5/16$-inch hologram eyes, 3D stick-on, red
Thread: Flat waxed nylon, red

Prey Species: Mullet
Fly Pattern: Steve's Snook Fly (white)
Fly Type: Impressionistic

TIER: STEVE VENINI

Hook: Mustad 34007, size 2/0
Wing: White marabou, over which is pearl Flashabou
Collar: White bucktail
Head: Spun white bucktail, spun red bucktail, trimmed to shape
Eyes: $5/16$-inch hologram eyes, 3D stick-on, silver
Thread: Flat waxed nylon, red

Prey Species: Mullet
Fly Pattern: MirroLure Fly
Fly Type: Impressionistic

TIER: CRAIG SMOTHERS

Hook: Gamakatsu B10S Stinger, size 1/0
Tail: Four to six matched white neck feathers, four to six strands of opal Flashabou Mirage
Collar: White Arctic fox body hair
Body: White and red spun deer body hair
Eyes: 5-millimeter 3D eyes
Thread: Flymaster + 3/0, white
Tier Comments: Top-water fishing is always exciting! Glue the eyes on with Fletch-Tite (used for archery), the best material for attaching eyes quickly and permanently.

SECTION VI
Miscellaneous Bottom Prey

CHAPTER 29

Segmented Worms
Polychaeta

Prey Type: Bottom-dwelling worms
Primary Habitats: Most coastal habitats used by gamefish; most species of concern here live in or on soft bottom or among oyster shells.
Geographic Range: Warm-temperate, subtropical, and tropical regions
Comments: Polychaetes are found in most coastal habitats and find their shelter from many gamefish by living in the bottom. Many are filter feeders (filtering plankton and other material from the water); some prey on other small organisms living in and on the bottom; and others feed on organic matter. Bonefish, red drum, and other fish that often feed on the bottom will try to dig, slurp, or excavate polychaetes from their burrows. Many times gamefish will grab and bite off the top portion of the polychaete that is near or extending from the surface. This portion eventually grows back.

The major exception to their bottom-dwelling existence for some species is when they emerge en masse to spawn. These spawning events tend to take place near new or full moons, often early or late in the day in low-light conditions. As with many species, during spawning caution is thrown to the wind. This makes for a great feeding opportunity for gamefish—from striped bass in New England to tarpon in the Florida Keys.

Numerous species of polychaetes are eaten by gamefish. Bloodworm types, one of the most commonly encountered species, are shown here.

Species: Bloodworm type

Primary Habitats: Mostly soft bottom habitats, also within the sediment in oyster bars
Geographic Range: Tropical, subtropical, and warm-temperate regions
Size Range: to 3 or 4 inches
Comments: Among other attributes, some species are the polychaetes of the famous "worm hatches," swimming to the water surface en masse to spawn. These "hatches" are targeted by tarpon in the Florida Keys and striped bass in New England.

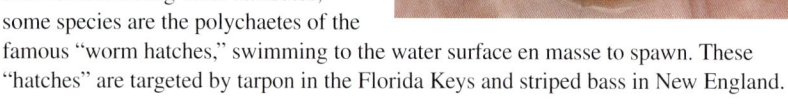

Photo on page 181: Potholes (open areas) in seagrass beds offer a good opportunity to fish weighted flies on the bottom.

The species are all very similar in appearance, so the flies below should be equally applicable. This type of polychaete is high on the menu of small bonefish (less than 16 inches) feeding on soft bottom and, at times, of red drum. Polychaetes are able to stretch and compress at will. When free-swimming, typical length is approximately 3 inches.

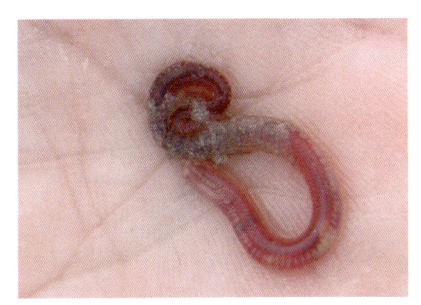

FLIES

Prey Species: Palolo Worm
Fly Pattern: Palolo Worm
Fly Type: Impressionistic

TIER: CHRIS DEAN

Hook: Mustad 9175, size 3/0
Tail: Tan rabbit strip barred with a red marker, $2^1/_2$ inches long
Tail support: 40-pound-test Mason monofilament loop
Body: Tan chenille
Thread: Flat waxed nylon, white

Segmented Worm Flies

Tier Comments: I don't know who designed this fly that I found on the Internet. This is one of the patterns that I use for big tarpon on the ocean side of the Florida Keys. The fly is tied larger than the real palolo worms to be proportional to the hook, but the fly can be tied smaller for fishing the "worm hatch."

Prey Species: Polychaete
Fly Pattern: Clam Worm
Fly Type: Impressionistic

TIER: AARON ADAMS

Hook: Owner 5170-12, size 2/0
Tail: Burnt orange zonker strip
Body: Medium-orange medium chenille and burnt orange zonker strip palmered
Thread: Flat waxed nylon, orange
Tying Tips: The zonker strip and chenille are both tied in at the hook bend and palmered together so that they lay side-by-side rather than the zonker strip over the chenille. This gives the body a more segmented appearance.
Tier Comments: This pattern has done well in numerous situations where swimming polychaetes were present.

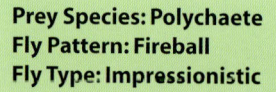

Prey Species: Polychaete
Fly Pattern: Fireball
Fly Type: Impressionistic

TIER: AARON ADAMS

Hook: Owner 5170-12, size 2/0
Tail: Red rabbit strip
Tail Support: Straight 40-pound-test monofilament, pierced through rabbit skin
Body: Medium-orange medium chenille, marked with black Sharpie
Hackle: Palmered red saddle hackle
Thread: Flat waxed nylon, orange
Tier Comments: This pattern has done well in numerous situations where swimming polychaetes were present. It gets its name from the obnoxious brightness that softens under water.

MISCELLANEOUS BOTTOM PREY

Prey Species: Polychaete
Fly Pattern: Chenille Sandworm
Fly Type: Imitation

TIER: AARON ADAMS

Hook: Mustad 34007, size 2 or 4
Tail and Body: Red medium chenille
Anti-foul: Loop of 20-pound-test monofilament tied in at the hook bend to keep the tail from wrapping around the hook bend
Thread: Flat waxed nylon, red

Prey Species: Polychaete
Fly Pattern: Light Wiggle Worm
Fly Type: Imitation

TIER: JACK GARTSIDE

Hook: Mustad 34011, sizes 2 to 1/0
Tail: Orange-tan Wiggle Worm (or Bohemian) chenille
Hackle: Narrow orange-rust dyed grizzly
Body: Orange-tan Wiggle Worm (or Bohemian) chenille
Head: Dubbed and picked-out mix of black-orange-brown blended dubbing, with a little peacock blaze GSS mixed in as well
Thread: Danville 3/0 monocord, brown or black
Tier Comments: The Wiggle Worm shown here imitates the numerous seaworm (also called sandworm or clamworm) species found throughout the year on most mud flats, mussel beds, and in many other areas where they become prey for stripers and other gamefish. These worms are not to be confused with the epitoke stage of the spawning sandworm, which many anglers are aware of as the "worm hatch." These latter are quite different in color, size, and configuration. This very simple fly has become one of my recent favorites to fish, and I recommend it as a worthy addition to your fly-fishing arsenal. It is tied with a super-soft, two-strand, very plush chenille that I call Wiggle Worm chenille. It is sold by some craft stores and fly-tying suppliers under various names.

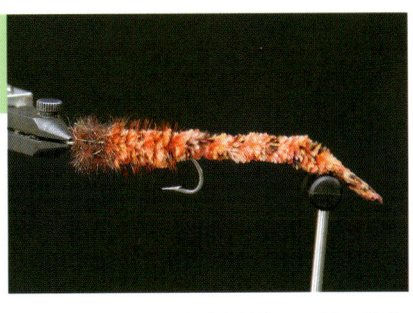

Segmented Worm Flies

Prey Species: Polychaete
Fly Pattern: Dark Worm Gurgler
Fly Type: Impressionistic

TIER: JACK GARTSIDE

Hook: Mustad 34011, sizes 2 to 1/0
Tail: Brown-black Wiggle Worm (or Bohemian) chenille
Hackle: Narrow orange-rust dyed grizzly
Body: Brown-black Wiggle Worm (or Bohemian) chenille
Back: Double-layered (tan over black) $1/8$-inch fly foam, tied Gurgler-style
Thread: Danville 3/0 monocord, brown or black
Tier Comments: This is a good pattern for when the spawning polychaetes are swimming near the surface and are being fed upon by gamefish.

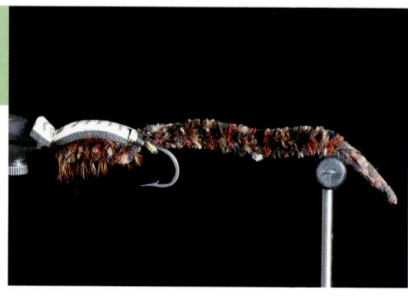

CHAPTER 30

Sea Urchins
Echinoidea

Prey Type: Bottom-associated prey
Primary Habitats: Rocky and rubble bottom areas
Geographic Range: Tropics
Comments: This is most certainly an untapped prey group for fly anglers. Admittedly, urchin flies are tough to fish—no stripping for these bottom-dwelling species—but they are eaten enough by permit and bonefish that flies to imitate these prey really should be more common. I've found that bonefish and permit feed on urchins when in rubble and beachrock shoreline habitats. If urchins are present, you'll quickly find out—by picking up a few pieces of rubble, you'll find small urchins on the underside or will see the short spines sticking out from crevices on beachrock shorelines.

Species: *Echinometra* spp

(numerous species that vary in color)

Primary Habitats: These urchins are common in crevices of rubble-bottomed flats and beachrock shorelines.
Geographic Range: Tropics
Size Range: Body to 2 inches in diameter, usually smaller
Comments: Urchins are very slow moving and remain tight in crevices or under rubble during the day. However, they do occasionally get dislodged or aren't hidden quite well enough, and in these instances are eaten by permit and bonefish. If they are abundant, you will be able to see urchin spines poking from their hiding places. There are numerous species in this genus, each with slightly different coloration, but all are similar in size.

FLIES

Prey Species: Urchin
Fly Pattern: Kushball
Fly Type: Impressionistic

TIER: AARON ADAMS

Hook: Mustad 34007, size 4
Body: Black rubber legs, tied to the hook at the center of the hook shank, splayed out when thread is tightened
Weight: Dumbbell eyes (optional, for use in water more than 2 feet deep)
Thread: Danville flat waxed nylon, black
Weedguard: 30-pound-test Ande monofilament
Tier Comments: This pattern can also be tied in red or other colors to match local urchins. I learned how important sea urchins are in the diet of permit when living on St. Croix—small nickel- or quarter-size urchins were the preferred live bait when spin fishing—and after numerous attempts at complex imitations, this simple pattern proved to be the best. I also occasionally use a fly of a single bunch of black or purple deer hair, spun and clipped as a sphere. The fly must be cast close enough to the fish for the fish to see it slowly drop to the bottom. Make sure you have a tight line, because the take is usually subtle.

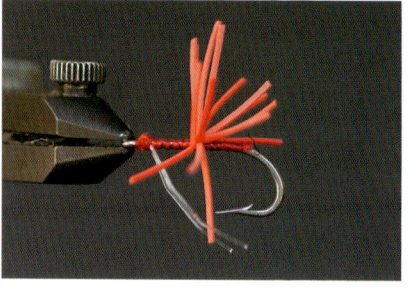

MISCELLANEOUS BOTTOM PREY

LIST OF FLY TIERS

AARON ADAMS
Aaron holds master's and Ph.D. degrees in marine and environmental science, in addition to a captain's license, and has studied marine fish ecology throughout his professional career. A lifelong angler, Aaron had the great fortune of cutting his fly-fishing teeth on the flats of the Virgin Islands while working there as a fish biologist. These skills served him well while pursuing striped bass and bluefish on the flats of Cape Cod during his four years living near Boston, where he also tied flies commercially for local shops and anglers. Aaron's current home waters are in and around Charlotte Harbor, on Florida's southwest coast. His career as a fish ecologist takes him to various locations in the Caribbean, and he packs a fly rod on most research trips. He is author of *Fisherman's Coast*, wrote four chapters for Chico Fernández's *Fly-Fishing for Bonefish*, has written numerous articles for fly-fishing magazines, and has given many seminars on fish ecology for anglers in numerous venues. He is presently the manager of the Fisheries Habitat Ecology Program at Mote Marine Lab and is director of operations and research for Bonefish & Tarpon Unlimited.

GINGER ALLEN
Ginger is a biological scientist for the University of Florida during the week, but she and her husband Chuck love to fly-fish the Florida backcountry on weekends. Ginger began fishing before she could tie her shoes and began tying flies while studying aquatic systems at the University of Montana in the 1980s. Ginger loves to diversify: By learning how to tie traditional classic salmon streamers to the latest synthetic marvels, she has become a very inventive tier. In the mid-1990s Ginger began experimenting with saltwater fly patterns. She teaches a salt/warmwater tying class at Lee Island Outfitters Orvis shop in Fort Myers, Florida. Ginger is a member of the Federation of Fly Fishers, International Women's Fly Fishers, and International Women's Fishing Association. She is also a professional staff member of Whiting Farms, Mustad, Gudebrod, Dyna King, Fishient, and Loon Products. Ginger has demonstrated her fly-tying techniques on local TV programs, at shallow water expos, International Fly-Tying Symposiums, and Fly-Fishing Retailer Expos. She is also a board discussion leader for *Fly Tyer* magazine.

KEN BAY
Ken lived on Long Island, New York, when he learned to tie flies in the early 1950s under the tutelage of local icon Herb Howard (remember Danville's Herb Howard Thread?), and he fished the Catskill Mountain streams for many years. Ken soon discovered a Saltwater Fly Rodders chapter near his home and began his saltwater fly-fishing career about 1960. In 1974, the Federation of Fly Fishers named him "fly tier of the year" and granted

him life membership. Other activities included membership in the Striped Bass Fund in 1975 and president of the Theodore Gordon Flyfishers, NYC, in 1975–76. During these years he authored three fly tying books: *Salt Water Flies* (1972); *How to Tie Freshwater Flies* (1974); and *American Fly Tyers Handbook* (1979). He retired from business in New York City in 1977 and moved to Florida in 1989. He currently teaches a fly-tying class sponsored by the Mid-coast Flyfishers in Daytona Beach, Florida.

TOM BERRY

Tom, a Federation of Fly Fishers (FFF) life member has tied flies at the FFF International Conclave, the Angling Fair in England, the Sowbug Roundup, the Southern and Southeastern conclaves, and has had his flies and ideas featured in numerous fly-tying books and magazines and on national television. Being an innovative fly tier, he has developed a series of saltwater flies called Breakthrough Flies, which include spoons, squids, minnows, shrimp, and crabs. These flies, which are practically indestructible, are not only beautiful, but catch fish! (Tom was able to contribute his fly patterns to the book despite losing his home to hurricane Katrina and being somewhat of a nomad for much of the time since.)

GORDON CHURCHILL

From the trout streams of Upstate New York to the coast of North Carolina is a long way by car. Even further by fly rod. Making the transition from 4-weight and size 18 dries to 8-weight and size 1/0 crab flies is not just a physical journey but a metaphysical one as well. Casting a fly to a fish you know is there is what it's all about. To actually be able to see the fish before you cast is even better. Gordon lives for that. In Upstate New York and specifically in the Delaware River branches, this is understood. In North Carolina when you tell other anglers that you spent all morning poling grass flats and casting to tailing fish and only caught two, you get a funny look and a patronizing tone of voice, "That sounds like . . . fun." With a master's degree in physical education, Gordon became a fly-fishing guide. It gives Gordon a real insight on breaking down physical skills and helping folks improve whatever it is they want to get better at—even casting a fly to tailing redfish. Gordon's advice to all who pursue such things is to not put your name on the side of your boat and find flats in the backs of creeks behind stands of tall pine trees. Go to www.flyfish-nc.com to get an idea.

MARSHALL CUTCHIN

Marshall guided fly fishers in the lower Florida Keys from 1985 until 1997, specializing in permit and tarpon. He now publishes the fly-fishing Web site www.MidCurrent.com.

CHRIS DEAN

Chris started fly fishing and tying flies in 1961, when he and his family lived on the Coral Gables Waterway in Miami. He spent most evenings after school fishing for snook, baby tarpon, and jacks. On weekends his mother dropped him off at the beach, where he could wade a small flat and fish for barracuda and the occasional bonefish. Chris taught himself how to cast a fly rod and tie flies by trial and error and by reading books and magazine articles, especially those by Joe Brooks. While he was growing up, his family occasionally had boats that he used to get to flats where he waded with a fly rod. During periods without a family boat, Chris found places he could access from land, including Tamiami Trail for snook and baby tarpon, and Upper Keys flats for bonefish. Chris graduated from the University of Miami in 1971 with a B.S. in biology, and after two years in the Army he worked in the medical science field until turning fishing and tying flies into a career.

OSCAR FELIU

Oscar began fishing in the streams of his native Chile. He studied entomology and conducted aquatic studies in Michigan streams and was a resident of Michigan for twenty years. He has been an innovative fly tier for over twenty-eight years and has conducted demonstrations and workshops throughout the United States, Canada, and Italy. A member of the Federation of Fly Fishers, he has conducted workshops and demonstrations at the annual FFF International Show. Oscar has also been featured in numerous magazines and fly-tying books.

BUZ FENDER

Buz grew up in Michigan and has fished forever but began fly fishing about fifteen years ago. He now spends summers fly-fishing streams and for "Golden Bones" (large carp that cruise the shoals of northern Lake Michigan). He spends winters in southwest Florida, fishing estuaries. He is a member of the Federation of Fly Fishers (FFF), the Adams chapter of Trout Unlimited, and the Caloosa Fly Fishers of southwest Florida.

LES FULCHER

Les was raised in Florida and the Panama Canal Zone and graduated from Florida State University. He currently lives on Longboat Key, Sarasota, Florida. In addition to fishing his home waters around Sarasota, he also frequently travels to the Florida Keys to tangle with tropical gamefish. A longstanding member of the Sarasota County Fire Department, he plans to retire soon and do more fishing.

JACK GARTSIDE

Jack Gartside is one the most innovative, prolific, and inventive fly tiers of the modern era. He got his first fly-tying lesson in 1956 from Ted Williams, the great Boston Red Sox outfielder. Ever since he's been tying and fishing, accumulating an extraordinary range of fishing experience in fresh and salt water. He was one of the first fly tiers profiled in *Sports Illustrated* magazine (October 12, 1982). Jack's best-known original patterns include the Gurgler, Sparrow, Soft Hackle Streamer, and the Gartside Pheasant Hopper. His designs have been featured in Eric Leiser's *Book of Fly Patterns*, Judith Dunham's *The Art of the Trout Fly*, Lefty Kreh's *Salt Water Fly Patterns*, Dick Stewart's *Salt Water Flies*, and Dick Brown's *Flyfishing for Bonefish*. Jack has also authored numerous books.

JERRY GOLDSMITH

Jerry Goldsmith's earliest memories include sitting on the rocks in the early morning at Sakonnet Point in Little Compton, Rhode Island. The lantern would burn, the cocoa was hot, and the anticipation of a striper swallowing the eel on his hook started a lifelong passion for all things fishing. For the past thirty years, he has explored and fished the east and west coasts of central Florida with an 8-weight fly rod. Jerry is an accomplished fly fisherman and tier. He also ties at a fly-fishing shows and conclaves and is an occasional contributor to local fishing periodicals and Web sites. Most of his trips are now done by kayak.

DOUG HEDGES
Doug got his first taste of fly fishing in his early teenage years on family camping trips to the mountains of Colorado. Moving from the Western U.S. to Connecticut in his early twenties introduced him to saltwater fly fishing, and he has never really been the same since. The aggressive and blistering fight of bluefish and striped bass opened a whole new world to him. From Connecticut, schooling and employment changes took him to the Upper Midwest, where he pursued trout, salmon, steelhead, pike, and bass with a fly rod. Never completely shaking the urge to fly-fish in saltwater, trips were made to exotic locations in search of bonefish, before moving to Florida in 2001. Doug has now found a home fishing for tarpon, snook, redfish, and generally any gamefish that will eat flies in southern Florida.

ANDRIJ HORODYSKY
Andrij describes himself as literally a fishing freak, donning the multiple hats of passionate fly fisherman, obsessed fly tier, and aspiring fisheries biologist. He has been tying flies commercially for over a decade and has been a Signature Fly Designer for Umpqua Feather Merchants since 2001. Several of his bonefish patterns have appeared at numerous fly shops, mail-order vendors, and in the Cabela's catalog. His tying philosophy and Virginia Institute of Marine Science Ph.D. research reflect a lifelong fascination with vision and perception. His present research focuses on the interaction between visual and feeding ecology of estuarine gamefish. His fascination with how gamefish see the world and what they eat extends to the vise—vision is unquestionably the most vital sense for the fly fisherman to manipulate. His patterns, much like the prey they are designed to emulate, are a balance between form and function; a synergy of realism, movement, and purpose. He feels that patterns must attain the correct posture and look right when still, but exude lifelike qualities—prominent eyes, fanning mouthparts, quivering legs, nervous fins, impressions of segmentation and articulation. Nearly all of his flies employ natural or synthetic light-manipulating materials to give the impression of movement.

CHRIS HUMPHREY
Chris grew up fishing in south Florida. He caught his first fish when he was three and has been in love with the water, environment, and fishing ever since. After school, he moved to the Keys and worked for a large fly shop. He was so taken by fly fishing for saltwater gamefish that he taught himself how to fly-fish with a rod he made from a blank. Shortly after that, he caught his first bonefish on the fly, taken by a shrimp epoxy original. He became a research manager, which afforded him the time and place to hone his fly fishing. He now resides in Naples and teaches high school marine science and passes on his love for the water, environment, and fly fishing. He continues to tie for friends in the Keys and himself.

MIKE MARSILI
Mike grew up fishing along the New Jersey coast. By the late 1980s, he began fly fishing for striped bass, blue fish, and tuna. Not long after picking up a fly rod, Mike began tying his own flies. In 1999, Mike decided to expand his horizons and moved to south Florida, where he is now a guide, fishing the flats, backcountry, and offshore waters of Key Largo and the Bahamas for a range of gamefish, including bonefish, tarpon, snook, sailfish, marlin, and tuna.

TONY PETRELLA
During the past thirty years, Capt. Tony Petrella has conducted scores of fly-fishing and fly-casting clinics ranging in scope from absolute basics to intricate advanced-level techniques. He has created many fly patterns that are sold commercially and is a Coast Guard–licensed captain who guides anglers in Michigan and southwest Florida. He also is a former newspaper and magazine writer, editor, and publisher who presently writes for *Fly Fisherman* magazine, *Michigan's Streamside Journal, The Waterline,* and *Midwest Fly Fishing* magazine.

Based in northern Michigan on the headwaters of the famed Manistee River and southwest Florida on the Gulf of Mexico in Venice, his fishing adventures have taken him to many of the famous (and also some secret) rivers, streams, and bonefish flats of North America. He's chased virtually every gamefish that swims, from trout to tarpon—with a liberal dose of steelhead and salmon, hungry bass, and vicious pike thrown in for good measure.

GLENN PITTARD
Glenn's education as a saltwater angler began along the Outer Banks of North Carolina. His favorite activity is sight-casting to shallow water gamefish wherever they can be found. His home waters are in and around Sanibel, Captiva Island, and Pine Island Sound. He enjoys the variety of fish available and access to the Gulf of Mexico, which provides blue-water fly-fishing opportunities. He also enjoys traveling to fishing destinations at home and in the Bahamas. Within a three-hour drive of his home he can do it all, the Upper Keys for bonefish and permit, the Everglades canals for snook and juvenile tarpon, Florida's East Coast and the mullet run, Miami–Dade County and peacock bass, shad fishing on the St. John's River. There are so many great fly-fishing opportunities in the state of Florida, he doesn't see how he could ever move.

DAVE SKOK
Dave Skok is a Boston-based fly tier, photographer, and writer with twenty years of fresh and saltwater fly-fishing experience. He is a two-time winner of the Martha's Vineyard Striped Bass and Bluefish Derby and was lucky enough to be the only fly fisherman in the near-sixty year history of the Derby to win the Grand Prize. He has held the IGFA 6-pound tippet record for Atlantic Bonito since 1994. Dave's skill with rod, vise, pen, and camera has been featured in over a half-dozen books including Bob Veverka's *Innovative Saltwater Flies* (Stackpole Books, 1999) and numerous periodicals including *Field & Stream, Fish & Fly, Fly Fisherman, Fly Fishing in Saltwaters, Fly Fishing & Tying Journal, Saltwater Fly Fishing* and *Salt Water Sportsman,* among others.

CRAIG SMOTHERS

Craig has undergraduate degrees in English and ecology/biology, and a postgraduate degree in ornithology. In what he describes as his former life, he was a field research biologist/DNR officer. He has worked for Seascape Aquarium for more than twenty years, caring for large saltwater aquariums in homes and offices in west-central Florida. He cut his fly-fishing teeth on smallmouth bass and bream but now is most happy fishing for redfish.

Craig has been tying for local fly shops and guides for over fifteen years. He is a charter member of the Mangrove Coast Fly Fishers (current board member), a member of the Tampa Bay Fly Fishers and Federation of Fly Fishers, and long time tier at the Sarasota Fly Tyers.

STEVE VENINI

Steve is a native of Oregon and grew up fishing trout, salmon, and steelhead. In the mid-1970s, he moved to Idaho, gaining access to many of the great western rivers in Idaho, Wyoming, and southwest Montana. In those days fly shops were few and far between, so most fly fishermen had to learn to tie or do without, which led to creative trading with hunters and the use of a great array of road-kill to come up with materials to match the hatch. Steve moved to south Florida in the early '80s and got his first exposure to saltwater fly fishing. He's been guiding in the upper Florida Keys, Bahamas, and Caribbean since 1985 and has spent ten years on the blue marlin tournament circuit. Now he splits his time between his charter boat *Bonechance*, fly fishing the Key Largo and Everglades National Park area, and as a private guide for Bonefish & Tarpon Unlimited founder Tom Davidson.

RON WINN

Ron is a longtime resident of the central east coast of Florida, growing up in the small beach community of Indialantic in the 1950s and '60s. It wasn't long after he was introduced to fly fishing as a young adult that he tried his luck in the surf, his favorite environment. After having countless bucktails and streamers destroyed by toothy gamefish, Ron began using macramé fibers for a more durable fly. This approach to tying saltwater flies followed use of polypropylene fibers in kingfish lures in the 1960s and '70s (called "bugs"). Ron noticed that macramé available at craft stores was simply smaller diameter polypropylene. Once combed out, the fibers made for a lifelike and durable fly. Winn's Mac Mullet and Mac Pilchard flies are so named for their use of macramé. Today, many other synthetic materials are available in more colors and finer diameters.

BIBLIOGRAPHY

Abele, A. G., and W. Kim. "An Illustrated Guide to the Marine Decapod Crustaceans of Florida." State of Florida, Department of Environmental Protection. Technical Series, 8, no. 1, parts 1 and 2. Tallahassee, FL: 1986.

Adams, A. J. *Fisherman's Coast: An Angler's Guide to Marine Warm-water Gamefish and Their Habitats.* Mechanicsburg, PA: Stackpole Books, 2004.

Anonymous. "Spotted Seatrout." *North Carolina Division of Marine Fisheries Publication.*

———. "Red Drum." *North Carolina Division of Marine Fisheries Publication.*

Arrivillaga, A., and D. Baltz. "Comparison of Fishes and Macroinvertebrates of Seagrass and Bare-Sand Sites on Guatemala's Atlantic Coast." Bulletin of Marine Science 65, no. 2 (1999): 301–19.

Austin, H. M. "A Survey of the Ichthyofauna of the Mangroves of Western Puerto Rico during December 1967 – August 1968." *Caribbean Journal of Science* 111–12 (1971): 27–39.

Baelde, P. "Differences in the Structures of Fish Assemblages in *Thalassia testudinum* Beds in Guadeloupe, French West Indies, and Their Ecological Significance." *Marine Biology* 105 (1990): 163–73.

Baltz, D., J. Fleeger, C. F. Rakocinski, and J. N. McCall. "Food, Density, and Microhabitat: Factors Affecting Growth and Recruitment Potential of Juvenile Saltmarsh Fishes." *Environmental Biology of Fishes* 53 (1998): 89–103.

Blewett, D. A., R. A. Hensley, and P. W. Stevens. "Feeding Habits of Common Snook, *Centropomus undecimalis*, in Charlotte Harbor, Florida." *Gulf and Caribbean Research* 18 (2006): 1–14.

Bologna, P. A. X., and K. L. Heck Jr. "Macrofaunal Associations with Seagrass Epiphytes Relative Importance of Trophic and Structural Characteristics." *Journal of Experimental Marine Biology and Ecology* 242 (1999): 21–39.

Boothby, R. N., and J. W. J. Avault. "Food Habits, Length-weight Relationship, and Condition Factor of the Red Drum (*Sciaenops ocellata*) in Southeastern Louisiana." Transactions of the American Fisheries Society 2 (1971): 290–95.

Bortone, S. A., ed. *Biology of the Spotted Seatrout.* Boca Raton, FL: CRC Press,. 2003.

Boulon, R. H. J. "Use of Mangrove Prop Root Habitats by Fish in the Northern U.S. Virgin Islands." *Proceedings of the Gulf and Caribbean Fisheries Institute* 41 (1987): 189–204.

Brook, I. M. "Trophic Relationships in a Seagrass Community *Thalassia testudinum*, in Card Sound, Florida: Fish Diets in Relation to Macrobenthic and Cryptic Faunal Abundance." *Transactions of the American Fisheries Society* 1063 (1977): 219–29.

Bruger, G. E. "Age, Growth, Food Habits, and Reproduction of Bonefish, *Albula vulpes*, in South Florida Waters." *Florida Department of Natural Resources Marine Research Laboratory*. Research Publication 3 (1974).

Carmona-Suarez, C. A., and J. E. Conde. "Local Distribution and Abundance of Swimming Crabs *Callinectes* spp. and *Arenaeus cribrarius* on a Tropical Sand Beach." *Fisheries Bulletin* 100 (2002): 11–25.

Catano, S., and J. Garzon-Ferreira. "Ecologia Trofica del Sabalo *Megalops atlanticus* (Pisces: Megalopidae) en el Area de Cienega Grande de Santa Marta, Caribe Colombiano." *Revista de Biologia Tropical* 42, no. 3 (1994): 673–84.

Chaverri, D. C. "Ecologia Basica y Alimentacion del Sabalo (*Megalops atlanticus*) (Pisces: Megalopidae)." *Revista Biologia Tropical* 42, nos. 1–2 (1994): 225–32.

Colton, D. E., and W. S. Alevizon. "Feeding Ecology of Bonefish in Bahamian Waters." *Transactions of the American Fisheries Society* 112 (1983): 178–84.

Cowper, S. W. "The Drift Algae Community of Seagrass Beds in Redfish Bay, Texas." *Contributions in Marine Science* 21 (1978): 125–32.

Crabtree, R. E., C. Stevens, D. Snodgrass, and F. J. Stengard. "Feeding Habitats of Bonefish, *Albula vulpes*, from the Waters of the Florida Keys." *Fishery Bulletin* 96 (1998): 754–66.

Diener, R. A., A. Inglis, and G. B. Adams. "Stomach Contents of Fishes from Clear Lake and Tributary Waters, a Texas Estuarine Area." *Contributions in Marine Science* 18 (1974): 7–17.

Divita, R., M. Creel, and P. F. Sheridan."Foods of Coastal Fishes during Brown Shrimp, *Penaeus aztecus*, Migration from Texas Estuaries (June–July 1981)." *Fishery Bulletin* 81 (1983): 396–404.

Duarte, L. O., and C. B. Garcia. "Diet of the Mutton Snapper *Lutjanus analis* (Cuvier) from the Gulf of Salamanca, Colombia, Caribbean Sea." *Bulletin of Marine Science* 65, no. 2 (1999): 453–65.

Durako, M. J., R. C. Phillips, and R. R. Lewis III. "Proceedings of the Symposium on Subtropical-tropical Seagrasses of the Southeastern United States." *Florida Marine Research Institute*. Research Publication 42, 1987.

Durako, M. J., M. D. Murphy, and K. D. Haddad. "Assessment of Fisheries Habitat: Northeast Florida." *Florida Marine Research Institute*. Research Publication 45, 1988.

Fay, C. W., R. J. Neves, and G. B. Pardue. "Species Profiles: Life Histories and Environmental Requirements of Coastal Fishes and Invertebrates (Mid-Atlantic) —Striped Bass." *U.S. Fish and Wildlife Service Biological Report* 82(11.8), U.S. Army Corps of Engineers, TR EL-82-4, 1983.

Fernández, J. M., and A. J. Adams. *Fly-fishing for Bonefish*. Mechanicsburg, PA: Stackpole Books, 2004.

Gosner, K. L. *A Field Fuide to the Atlantic Seashore*. Boston: Houghton Mifflin, 1978.

Greening, H. S., and R. J. Livingston. "Diel Variation in the Structure of Seagrass Associated Epibenthic Macroinvertebrate Communities." *Marine Ecology Progress Series* 7 (1982): 147–56.

Heck, K.L. Jr. "Comparative Species Richness, Composition, and Abundance of Invertebrates in Caribbean Seagrass *Thalassia testudinum*." *Marine Biology* 41 (1977): 335–48.

Heck, K. L. Jr., and T. A. Thoman. "Experiments on Predator-prey Interactions in Vegetated Aquatic Habitats." *Journal of Experimental Marine Biology and Ecology* 53 (1981):125–34.

Heck, K. L. Jr., and G. S. Wetstone. "Habitat Complexity and Invertebrate Species Richness and Abundance in Tropical Seagrass Meadows." *Journal of Biography* 4 (1977): 135–42.

Hill, J., J. W. Evans, and M. J. Van Den Avyle. "Species Profiles: Life Histories and Environmental Requirements of Coastal Fishes and Invertebrates (South Atlantic)—Striped Bass." *U.S. Fish and Wildlife Service Biological Report* 82(11.118), U.S. Army Corps of Engineers, TR EL-82-4, 1989.

Hindell, J. S., G. P. Jenkins, and M. J. Keough. "Variability in Abundances of Fishes Associated with Seagrass Habitats in Relation to Diets of Predatory Fishes." *Marine Biology* 136 (2000): 725–37.

Hoese, H. D., and Moore, R. H. *Fishes of the Gulf of Mexico*. 2nd ed. College Station: Texas A&M Press, 1998.

Humann, P. *Reef Creature Identification: Florida, Caribbean, Bahamas*. 2nd ed. Jacksonville, FL: New World Publications, 1994.

Kaplan, E. H. *A Field Guide to Southeastern and Caribbean Seashores*. Boston: Houghton Mifflin, 1988.

———. *A Field Guide to Coral Reefs: Caribbean and Florida*. Boston: Houghton Mifflin, 1982.

Kilby, J. D. "The Fishes of Two Gulf Coastal Marsh Areas of Florida." *Tulane Studies in Zoology* 2, no.8 (1955):175–247.

Lassuy, D. R. "Species Profiles: Life Histories and Environmental Requirements (Gulf of Mexico)—Gulf Menhaden." *U.S. Fish and Wildlife Service Division of Biological Services*, FWS/OBS-82(11.2), U.S. Army Corps of Engineers, TR EL-82-4, 1983.

Ley, J., C. L. Montague, and C. C. McIvor. "Food Habits of Mangrove Fishes: A Comparison along Estuarine Gradients in Northeastern Florida Bay." *Bulletin of Marine Science* 54, no. 30 (1994): 881–99.

Mense, D. J., and E. L. Wenner. "Distribution and Abundance of Early Life History Stages of the Blue Crab, *Callinectes sapidus*, in Tidal Marsh Creeks near Charleston, South Carolina." *Estuaries* 12, no. 3 (1989): 157–68.

Mercer, L. P. "Species Profiles: Life Histories and Environmental Requirements of Coastal Fishes and Invertebrates (Mid-Atlantic)—Weakfish." *U.S. Fish and Wildlife Service Biological Report* 82(11.109), 1989.

———. "A Biological and Fisheries Profile of Red Drum, *Sciaenops ocellatus*." *North Carolina Department of Natural Resources and Community Development*. Special Scientific Report 41, 1984.

Minello, T. J., and R. J. Zimmerman. "Selection for Brown Shrimp, *Penaeus aztecus*, as Prey by the Spotted Seatrout, *Cynoscion nebulosus*." *Contributions in Marine Science* 27 (1984): 159–67.

Moody, K. M. "The Role of Drift Macroalgae as a Predation Refuge or Foraging Ground for the Seagrass Fish, *Gobiosoma robustum*." Master's Thesis, Department of Biology, University of South Florida, 1996.

Mueller, K. W., G. D. Dennis, D. B. Eggleston, and R. I. Wicklund. "Size-specific Social Interactions and Foraging Styles in a Shallow Water Population of Mutton Snapper, *Lutjanus analis* (Pisces: Lutjanidae), in the Central Bahamas." *Environmental Biology of Fishes* 40 (1994): 175–88.

Mullin, S. J. "Estuarine Fish Populations among Red Mangrove Prop Roots of Small Overwash Islands." *Wetlands* 154 (1995): 324–29.

Murphey, P. L., and M. S. Fonseca. "Role of High and Low Energy Seagrass Beds as Nursery Areas for *Penaeus duorarum* in North Carolina." *Marine Ecology Progress Series* 121 (1995): 91–98.

Naughton, S. P., and C. H. Saloman. "Fishes of the Nearshore Zone of St. Andrew Bay, Florida, and Adjacent Coast." *Northeast Gulf Science* 21 (1978): 43–55.

Overstreet, R. M., and R. W. Heard. "Food of the Red Drum, *Sciaenops ocellata*, from Mississippi Sound." *Gulf Research Reports* 6, no. 2 (1978): 131–35.

Peters, D. J., and W. G. Nelson. "The Seasonality and Spatial Patterns of Juvenile Surf Zone Fishes of the Florida East Coast." *Florida Scientist* 50 (1987): 85–99.

Primavera, J. H. "Fish Predation on Mangrove-associated Penaeids: The Role of Structure and Substrate." *Journal of Experimental Marine Biology and Ecology* 215 (1997): 205–16.

Randall, J. E. "Food Habits of Reef Fishes of the West Indies." *Studies in Tropical Oceanography* 5 (1967): 665–847.

Reagan, R. E. "Species Profiles: Life Histories and Environmental Requirements of Coastal Fishes and Invertebrates (Gulf of Mexico)—Red Drum." *U.S. Fish and Wildlife Service Biological Report* 82(11.36), U.S. Army Corps of Engineers, TR EL-82-4, 1985

Robins, C. R., G. C. Ray, and J. Douglass. *A Field Guide to Atlantic Coast Fishes of North America.* Boston: Houghton Mifflin, 1986.

Rogers, S. G., and M. J. Van Den Avyle. "Species Profiles: Life Histories and Environmental Requirements of Coastal Fishes and Invertebrates (South Atlantic)—Atlantic Menhaden." *U.S. Fish and Wildlife Service, Division of Biological Services. Biological Report* FWS/OBS-82(11.11), U.S. Army Corps of Engineers, TR EL-82-4, 1983.

Savino, J. F., and R. A. Stein. "Behavior of Fish Predators and Their Prey: Habitat Choice between Open Water and Dense Vegetation." *Environmental Biology of Fishes* 24, no. 4 (1989): 287–93.

Scharf, F. S., and K. K. Schlicht. "Feeding Habits of Red Drum (*Sciaenops ocellatus*) in Galveston Bay, Texas: Seasonal Diet Variation and Predator-prey Size Relationships." *Estuaries* 23, no. 1 (2000): 128–39.

Schneider, F. I., and K. H. Mann. Species Relationships of Invertebrates to Vegetation in a Seagrass Bed." *Journal of Marine Biology and Ecology* 145 (1991): 101–17.

Seaman, W. Jr., and M. Collins. "Species Profiles: Life Histories and Environmental Requirements of Coastal Fishes and Invertebrates (South Florida)—Snook." *U.S. Fish and Wildlife Service* FWS/OBS-82(11.16), U.S. Army Corps, 1983.

Sedberry, G. R., and J. Carter. "The Fish Community of a Shallow Tropical Lagoon in Belize, Central America." *Estuaries* 162 (1993): 198–215.

Sheridan, P. F., D. L. Trimm, and B. M. Baker. "Reproduction and Food Habits of Seven Species of Northern Gulf of Mexico Fishes." *Contributions in Marine Science* 27 (1984): 175–204.

Wenner, C. D. "Red Drum: Natural History and Fishing Techniques in South Carolina." *South Carolina Department of Natural Resources*. Educational Report 17, 1992.

Wenner, C., and J. Archambault. "Spotted Seatrout: Natural History and Fishing Techniques in South Carolina." *South Carolina Department of Natural Resources*. Educational Report 18, 1995.

Whitehead, P. J. P., and R. Vergara. "Megalopidae." In *FAO Species Identification Sheets for Fishery Purposes, Western Central Atlantic (Fishery Area 31)*. Volume 3. Edited by W. Fischer. Rome: FAO, 1978.

Williams, A. B. *Shrimps, Lobsters, and Crabs of the Atlantic Coast of the Eastern United States, Maine to Florida*. Washington, DC: Smithsonian Institution Press, 1984.

A good general Internet reference for scientific information on fish is www.fishbase.org. On this Web site you can search for information on fish species by the scientific name. The resulting page provides a summary of knowledge for the species and links to additional information.

INDEX

Anchovies (*Engraulidae*)
  bay (*Anchoa mitchilli*), 137, 138
  Cuban (*Anchoa cubana*), 137
  dusky (*Anchoa lyolepis*), 137
  flies, 138–140
  habitats and range, 136
  striped (*Anchoa hepsetus*), 136–137, 138
Anchovy, 138
Angora Shrimp, 73
Atlantic Silverside, 143

Baitfish
  anchovies, 136–140
  herrings, 148–161
  mullets, 168–179
  needlefishes, halfbeaks, and ladyfish, 162–167
  silversides, 141–147
Bay Anchovy MOE, 138
Bay Whistler, 160
Bendback
  for killifish, 129
  for silversides, 142
Bendback Blenny, 94
Bendback Gurgler, 51
Bendback Pinfish, 110
Big Ugly, 60
Blennies (*Bleniidae*)
  crested (*Hypleurochilus geminatus*), 92
  feather (*Hypsoblennius hentzi*), 91, 92
  flies, 92–94
  Florida (*Chasmodes saburrae*), 90, 93
  habitats and range, 90
  hairy (*Labrisomus nuchipinnis*), 91
  striped (*Chasmodes bosquianus*), 91
  unidentified (*Labrisomus*), 91
Blind Crab, 42
Blueback Deceiver, 157
Blueback Herring, 161
Bonefish Joe, 37
Bonefish Special, 74
Bonito Deceiver, 144
Braided Needlefish Fly, 166
Bridled Goby, 87
Bristle Worm, 66
Broken-back shrimp (*Hippolytidae*)
  eelgrass (*H. zostericola*), 77
  flies, 78–82
  habitats and range, 76
Brown Gulf Shrimp, 51
Brown Recluse, 38
Bucktail Blonde, 139
Bunny Mantis, 65
Bunny Shrimp, 56
Buz's Long Shrimp, 66
Buz's Shrimp, 55
Buz's Snook Body Fly, 155
Buz's Snook Yak Fly, 156

Cactus Clouser, 52
Cactus Minnow, 146
Cactus Minnow Floater, 146
Charlie's Floating Crab, 12
Chenille Sandworm, 185
Chernobyl Shrimp, 53
ChiliPepper, 74
Cinnamon Shrimp, 79
Clam Worm, 184

Clouser Minnow
    chartreuse and white, for silversides, 145
    for grunts, 102
    for slippery Dick, 114
    tan or brown, for common shrimp, 52
Coker Smoker, 55
Common shrimp (*Penaeidae*)
    brown (*Farfantepenaeus aztecus*), 47, 50, 51
    flies, 48–58
    habitats and range, 46
    pink (*Farfantepenaeus duorarum*), 46, 48, 50
    white (*Litopenaeus setiferus*), 47
Conehead Blenny, 93
Conehead Mojarra, 119
Conehead Toad, 98
Corsair Minnow, 155
Crabs
    fiddler, 13–19
    mangrove and marsh, 9–12
    mole, 40–43
    mud, 2–8
    porcelain, 25
    spider, 20–24
    swimming, 26–39
Craft Fur Clouser
    chartreuse for gobies, 88–89
    tan or pink for snapping shrimp, 71
Crazy Charlie, 147
Crested Blenny Bunny, 92
Critter Crab, 7
Crystal Minnow, 145

Dark Worm Gurgler, 186
Dash Goby, 88
Dean Permit Crab, 35
Dean Redfish Fly, 54
Deerhair Mole Crab, 42
Deer-hair Mullet, 174
Del Brown's Merkin, 32
Delta Dart Minnow, 153
DH Shrimp, 50
Dime Crab, 33

Drums (*Sciaenidae*)
    croaker (*Micropogonias undulatus*), 106
    flies, 106
    habitats and range, 105
    kingfish (whiting) (*Menticirrhus* spp), 105, 106
    spot (*Leiostomus xanthurus*), 105
Dust Bunny, 82

EAP, 11
Edible Blue Crab, 33
Eels (*Anguillidae*)
    American (*A. rostrata*), 132
    flies, 132–133
    habitats and range, 132
Epoxy Forage, 140
Epoxy Mudbug, 72

Fantail Mullet Deceiver, 174
Feather Blenny Bunny, 92
Female Rosy Razorfish, 115
Fernández Snapping Shrimp, 73
Fiddler Crab, 19
Fiddler crabs (*Ocypodidae*), 13
    Burger's (*Uca burgersi*), 14
    Caribbean (*Uca rapax*), 14
    flies, 17–19
    ghost (*Ocypode quadrata*), 17
    habitats and range, 13
    Ive's (*Uca speciosa*), 14
    lavender (*Uca vocator*), 16
    long-wave Gulf (*Uca longisignalis*), 16
    mud (*Uca pugnax*), 15
    panacea sand (*Uca panacea*), 15
    red-jointed (*Uca minax*), 14
    sand (*Uca pugilator*), 15
    spined (*Uca spinicarpa*), 16
    Thayer's sand (*Uca thayeri*), 16
Fireball, 184
Fishair Silverside, 145
FisHead Sandeel, 133
Fleeing Crab, 36
Flexi-Mullet, 171

Floating Fleeing Crab, 36–37
Floating Pass Crab, 32
Florida Blenny Bunny, 93
Flyingfishes. *See* Halfbeaks and
    flyingfishes
Furback Snapping Shrimp, 75
Furry Mantis, 67
Fur Shrimp, 48

Ghost shrimp (*Callianassidae*)
    Atlantic (*C. atlantica*), 60
    flies, 60–61
    habitats and range, 59
    trilobed (*C. trilobata*), 60
    West Indian (*C. major*), 59
Glass Minnow, 139–140
Glenn's Glass Minnow, 144
Gobies (*Gobiidae*)
    bridled (*Coryphopterus
        glaucofraenum*), 86, 87
    clown (*Microgobius gulosus*), 84
    code (*Gobiosoma robustum*), 85
    dash (*Gobionellus saepepallens*), 86,
        88
    flies, 87–89
    frillfin (*Bathygobius soporator*), 85
    goldspot (*Gnatholepis thompsoni*),
        87, 88
    habitats and range, 84
    naked (*Gobiosoma bosci*), 85
    orangespotted (*Nes longus*), 86, 88
    rockcut (*Gobiosoma grosvenori*), 86
Golden Mantis, 65
Goldspot Goby, 88
Gordo's Glass Minnow, 143
Grass shrimp (*Palaemonidae*)
    flies, 78–82
    Florida (*P. floridana*), 77
    grass (*P. pugio*), 77
    habitats and range, 76
Grass Shrimp, 80–81
Gray Squirrel Bendback, 79
Green Mantis Shrimp, 64
Green Mud Crab, 6

Grizzly Bendback, 131
Grunts (*Haemulidae*)
    bluestriped (*H. sciurus*), 100
    flies, 101–102
    French (*H. flavolineatum*), 100
    habitats and range, 99
    pigfish (*Orthopristis chrysoptera*),
        100, 101
    white (*H. plumieri*), 99
Gulf Toadfish Conehead, 97
Gurgler, 170

Hackle Crab, 24
Hackle Muddler, 178
Hairball Fiddler, 18–19
Hairball Mole, 43
Halfbeaks and flyingfishes (*Exocoetidae*)
    Balao (*Hemiramphus balao*), 163
    flies, 166
    habitats and range, 163
    hardhead (*Chriodorus atherinoides*),
        164
Herrings (sardines) (*Clupeidae*)
    alewife (*Alosa pseudoharengus*), 149
    Atlantic thread (*Opisthonema
        oglinum*), 150, 152
    blueback (*Alosa aestivalis*), 150, 161
    flies, 151–161
    habitats and range, 148
    menhaden (*Brevoortia* spp), 150, 152,
        153
    redear sardine (*Harengula humeralis*),
        150
    scaled (*Harengula jaguana*), 149,
        151, 159, 160
    Spanish (*Sardinella aurita*), 149, 154
Hollow Deceiver, 153
Homosassa Deceiver, 167
Hophead, 56–57

Jerry's Critter, 8
Jerry's Mullet, 175
Juvenile Sardine, 154

KB Indian River Shrimp, 49
KB Pigfish Jr., 101
KB Pigfish Sr., 101
KB Pinfish, 108
Killifishes (*Cyprinodontidae*)
   bayou (*Fundulus pulvereus*), 126
   diamond (*Adinia xenica*), 123
   flies, 127–131
   goldspotted (*Floridichthys carpio*), 124
   Gulf (*Fundulus grandis*), 124
   habitats and range, 122
   longnose (*Fundulus similis*), 125, 128
   marsh (*Fundulus confluentus*), 125
   mummichug (*Fundulus heteroclitus*), 125, 127
   rainwater (*Lucania parva*), 123
   saltmarsh topminnow (*Fundulus jenkinsi*), 126
   sheepshead minnow (*Cyprinodon variegatus*), 123, 130
   spotfin (*Fundulus luciae*), 126
   striped (*Fundulus majalis*), 125
Kinky Fiber Anchovy, 140
Kinky Mangrove Minnow, 130
Krystal Shrimp, 48
Kushball, 188

Ladyfish (*Elopidae*)
   Elops saurus, 164
   flies, 167
   habitats and range, 164
Leech Shrimp, 54–55
Leftover Shrimp, 49
Lefty's Deceiver
   for grunts, 102
   for snappers, 104
Legless Merkin, 34
Light Wiggle Worm, 185
Longnose Killifish, 128

Mac Mullet, 173
Mac Pilchard or Greenie, 151
Male Rosy Razorfish, 115

Mangrove crabs (*Grapsidae*)
   habitats and range, 9
   flies, 10–11, 12
   tree (*Aratus pisonii*), 9
Mangrove Minnow, 128
Mangrove Muddler, 127
Mantis shrimp (*Squillidae*)
   common (*S. empusa*), 63
   flies, 64–67
   golden (*Pseudosquilla ciliata*), 63
   habitats and range, 62
   rock (*Gonodactylus oerstedii*), 62–63
Marabou Mole Crab, 43
Marabou Muddler, short and long versions, 176–177
Marabou Pass Crab, 31
Marabou Toad, 97
Marsh Crab, 12
Marsh crabs (*Grapsidae*)
   flies, 11–12
   gray (*Sesarma cinereum*), 10
   habitats and range, 9
   marbled (*Sesarma ricordi*), 10
   purple (*Sesarma reticulatum*), 10
McVay Gotcha, 71
Mega Mushy, 152
Merkin, 37–38
Merkin Spey, 34
Mike's Floating Crab, 39
Mini Assassin, 80
MirroLure Fly, 179
Mojarra Hi-Tie, 120
Mojarras (*Gerreidae*)
   bigeye mojarra (*Eucinostomus havana*), 118
   flies, 119–121
   habitats and range, 116
   mottled mojarra (*Eucinostomus lefroyi*), 117
   silver Jenny (*Eucinostomus gula*), 117, 119
   slender mojarra (*Eucinostomus jonesi*), 117
   spotfin mojarra (*Eucinostomus argenteus*), 117

striped mojarra (*Diapterus plumieri*), 118
tidewater mojarra (*Eucinostomus harengulus*), 118
yellowfin mojarra (*Gerres cinereus*), 118
Mole crabs (*Hippidae*)
  common (*Emerita talpoida*), 40, 42
  Cuban (*Hippa cubensis*), 41
  flies, 42–43
  habitats and range, 40
  Puerto Rican (*Emerita portoricensis*), 41
  purple surf (*Albunea gibbesii*), 41
  Webster's (*Lepidopa websteri*), 41
Mollies and mosquitofish (*Poeciliidae*)
  flies, 127
  habitats and range, 122
  sailfin (*Poecilia latipinna*), 126
Mosquitofish (*Gambusia holbrooki*), 126
  flies, 127
  habitats and range, 122
Mud Crab Pulverizer, 6
Mud crabs (*Xantidae*)
  common (*Panopeus herbstii*), 2
  denticulate (rubble) (*Xantho denticulata*), 4
  depressed (*Eurypanopeus depressus*), 3
  flies, 6–8
  Florida (*Cataleptodius floridanus*), 4
  habitats and range, 2
  narrow (*Hexapanopeus angustifrons*), 3
  Say's (*Neopanope sayi*), 3
  stone (*Menippe mercenaria*), 4
  Texas (*Neopanope texana*), 3
Mud shrimp (*Thalassinidae*)
  flies, 60–61
  habitats and range, 59
  mud (*Upogebia affinis*), 60
Mullet Deceiver, 172
Mullets (*Mugilidae*)
  fantail (*Mugil gyrans*), 169, 174
  flies, 170–179
  habitats and range, 168
  Liza (*Mugil liza*), 169
  striped (black) (*Mugil cephalis*), 168, 174, 175
  white (*Mugil curema*), 169
Mushmouth, 152

Needlefishes (*Belonidae*)
  flies, 165–166
  habitats and range, 162
  Strongylura spp, 162–163
Night Deceiver, 160
No-look Fiddler, 17–18
Norman's Crab, 22–23
Nylon Hair Halfbeak, 166
Nylon Hair Needlefish, short and long, 165

Olive and White Bendback, 131
Olive Clouser Minnow, 131
Olive Seaducer, 130
Orangespotted Goby, 88
Oscar's Beach Darter, 139
Oscar's Beach Dweller, 121
Oscar's Blue Darter, 158
Oscar's Herring, 158–159
Oscar's Ladyfish, 167
Oscar's Little Mullet, 178
Oscar's Mini-bait, 133
Oscar's Pinfish, 109
Oscar's Sardine, 159
Oscar's Threadfin, 158
Oscar's Whitebait, 159
Oyster Toadfish Conehead, 97

Palmered Hackle Shrimp, 78
Palolo Worm, 183–184
Parrotfishes (*Scaridae*)
  bucktooth (*Sparisoma radians*), 113
  flies, 114–115
  habitats and range, 112
Pass Crab Toad, 31
Pearly Razorfish, 114
Petrella's Blenny, 93
Petrella's Brown Goby, 89

Petrella's Champagne Goby, 89
Petrella's Crab, 11
Phat Phoam Gurgler, 170
Pilchard, 157
Pink Spey Shrimp, 50
Polar Fiber Minnow, 156
Polar Fiber Mullet, 173
Pompom Crab, for mud crabs, 7
Pom-pom Crab, for spider crabs, 23
Popovics's Jiggy, 138
Popovics's Siliclone, 175
Porcelain crabs (*Porcellanidae*)
   green (*Petrolisthes armatus*), 25
   habitats and range, 25
   lined (*Petrolisthes galathinus*), 25
Porgies (*Sparidae*)
   habitats and range, 107
   flies, 108–110
   pinfish (*Lagodon rhomboides*), 107
   sea bream (*Archosargus rhomboidalis*), 108
Purple Fiddler, 18

Real Thing, 56
Redfish Joe, 38
Ropp's Redfish Bendback, 57
RW Mantis Shrimp, 64

Sardines. See Herrings (*Clupeidae*)
Scrab, 18
Sea Trouter, 172
Sea urchins (*Echinoidea*)
   flies, 188
   habitats and range, 187
Secret Silverside, 147
Shrimp
   common, 46–58
   ghost and mud, 59–61
   grass and broken-back, 76–82
   mantis, 62–67
   snapping, 68–75
Silicone Finger Mullet, 176
Silver Jenny Streamer, 119
Silverside Rapala, 144

Silversides (*Atherinidae*)
   Atlantic (*Menidia menidia*), 142, 143, 144
   flies, 142–147
   habitats and range, 141
   hardhead (*Atherinomorus stripes*), 141
   inland (*Menidia beryllina*), 142
   tidewater (*Menidia peninsulae*), 141
Simple Snapping Shrimp, 75
Skok's Mushmouth Variant
   for herrings, 151
   for mojarra, 119
Slinky Hi-Tie, 161
Snappers (*Lutjanidae*)
   flies, 104
   habitats and range, 103
   mangrove (gray) (*Lutjanus griseus*), 104
   yellowtail (*Ocyurus chrysurus*), 103, 104
Snapping shrimp (*Alpheidae*)
   banded (*A. armillatus*), 68
   common (*A. heterochaelis*), 69
   flies, 71–75
   habitats and range, 68
   red (*A. armatus*), 69
   short-clawed sponge (*Synalpheus brevicarpus*), 70
   snapping (*A. bouvieri*), 69
   snapping (*A. estuariensis*), 69
   snapping (*A. paracrinitus*), 70
Spanish Sardine, 154
Sparkle Ugly, 61
Spider crabs (*Majidae*)
   coral (*Mithrax hispidus*), 22
   decorator (*Stenocionops furcata*), 21
   flies, 22–24
   gray pitho (*Pitho aculeata*), 22
   green reef (*Mithrax sculptus*), 21
   habitats and range, 20
   pitho (*Pitho mirabilis*), 21
   southern (*Libinia dubia*), 20
   tan reef (*Mithrax coryphe*), 22
Splat Crab, 10–11
Spun Shrimp, 78

Steve's Sheepshead Crab, 8
Steve's Snook Fly black and white, 179
Striped Mullet Seaducer, 175
Striped Mullet Streamer, 174
Sugarman Shrimp, 58
Swimming Crab, 35
Swimming crabs (*Portunidae*)
   blotched (*Portunus spinimanus*), 29
   blue (*Callinectes sapidus*), 27, 33
   Dana's blue (*Callinectes danae*), 28
   flies, 31–39
   habitats and range, 26
   iridescent (*Portunis gibbesii*), 28, 31, 32
   lady (*Ovalipes ocellatus*), 30, 34
   lesser blue (*Callinectes similis*), 27
   ornate blue (*Callinectes ornatus*), 28
   red-blue (*Callinectes bocourti*), 27
   Sargassum (*Portunus sayi*), 29
   speckled (*Arenaeus cribrarius*), 30

Tarpon Brown Shrimp, 50
Tarpon Shrimp, 52–53
Thread Herring, 154
Toadfish, 98
Toadfishes (*Batrachoididae*)
   Belize (*Opsanus* sp), 96
   flies, 96–98
   Gulf (*Opsanus beta*), 95, 97, 98
   habitats and range, 95
   oyster (*Opsanus tau*), 96, 97

Ugly Shrimp, 53
Ultra Shrimp, 81

Watch It Wiggle Bendback, 58
Whistler, 177
White Beach Fly, 119, 153
Whiting Half-and-Half, 106
Woolhead Goby, 87
Woolhead Whiting, 106
Woolly Bugger Goby, 89
Woolly Bugger Slider, 130
Woolly Mole, 42
Woolly Mummi, 127
Woolly Toad, 96
Wool Spider Crab, 24
Worms (*Polychaeta*)
   bloodworm type, 182–183
   flies, 183–186
   habitats and range, 182
Wrasses (*Labridae*)
   flies, 114–115
   habitats and range, 112
   pearly razorfish (*Hemipteronotus novacula*), 113, 114
   rosy razorfish (*Hemipteronotus martinicensis*), 113, 115
   slippery Dick (*Halichoeres bivittatus*), 112, 114

Zonker Eel, 132